THE BOOK OF
BOBBIN LACE STITCHES

Other books by Bridget Cook and Geraldine Stott:

100 Traditional Bobbin Lace Patterns
Geraldine Stott and Bridget M. Cook

The Bobbin Lace Manual
Geraldine Stott

Building Torchon Lace Patterns
Bridget M. Cook

Introduction to Bobbin Lace Patterns
Bridget M. Cook

Practical Skills in Bobbin Lace
Bridget M. Cook

Russian Lace Making
Bridget M. Cook

Russian Lace Patterns
Bridget M. Cook and Anna Korableva

The Torchon Lace Workbook
Bridget M. Cook

Visual Introduction to Bucks Point Lace
Geraldine Stott

THE BOOK OF
BOBBIN LACE
STITCHES

BRIDGET M. COOK & GERALDINE STOTT

Dover Publications, Inc.
Mineola, New York

First published 1980. Second edition 1982; reprinted 1984, 1987, 1993
and 1996. Revised and updated in paperback 2002

„ *Bridget M. Cook & Geraldine Stott* 1980 and 2002

International Standard Book Number 0-486-42228-3

Published in the United States and Canada by Dover Publications, Inc.

Printed in Spain

B T Batsford
64 Brewery Road
London N7 9NT
England
www.batsford.com

A member of the Chrysalis Group plc

INTRODUCTION

This book has been designed as a reference text book for the guidance of the growing number of bobbin lace makers across the full ability range.

Each page is devoted to just one of the many complex stitches and illustrates the completed stitch together with an enlargement. Then follows a diagrammatic drawing with the appropriate associated illustration followed by a graph of the pricking and the number of bobbins required.

The stitches are arranged according to their degree of difficulty with the simpler stitches appearing early on, progressing through to the more complex stitches. Towards the end are 'Spiders', 'Buds', 'Shells', 'Toiles' and 'Peas'.

It is to be hoped that the book will assist lace makers in widening their repertoire of stitches and enable them to develop their own free design as well as to use traditional prickings with a greater degree of flexibility.

Most of the stitches date from the late seventeenth or early eighteenth century when bobbin lace techniques were developed to their full potential. At that time the same or very similar stitches could be found in lace from widely separated countries and even districts within these countries. It is not surprising that similar stitches are known by different names dating from that period.

During the second half of the nineteenth century lace makers were relearning the complicated stitches lost during the neo-classical period and new names were applied. Some were purely descriptive, some were based on the antique laces from which the stitches were taken, some were based on institutions where lace making was practised and some were given totally new names, while other stitches were newly created. Lace makers from different areas will have a different vocabulary based in the main on these nineteenth-century names.

Lace makers will therefore appreciate the problems relating to the naming of the stitches in this book and the authors hope that they will be able to identify them satisfactorily. However it is the ability to execute the stitch that is important rather than simply knowing its name.

All samples have deliberately been made in a thick thread (Barbours No. 50 Linen) in order to show the construction of the stitches with greater clarity. In the same way the prickings have all been drawn to match this thickness. It is envisaged that the lace maker will be able to adjust the size quite simply by using a larger or smaller graph paper to suit the thread. For example, if 10 to 1 cm square graph paper is used then D.M.C. No. 60 Retors D'Alsace works quite well, but a sampler must be worked with the thread and graph paper intended for use.

As far as Bucks Point is concerned this again has been drawn to suit the graph paper (approximately 56°). However, it can be made at any angle from 45° to 68° according to the need.

Throughout the book all graphs have been drawn to the same scale. The photograph at the bottom left of each page is actual size, and has been made on the graph shown (10 to 1 inch), while that at the top left is an enlargement.

The numbers at the top of each graph relate to the number of *pairs* of bobbins needed for that particular stitch.

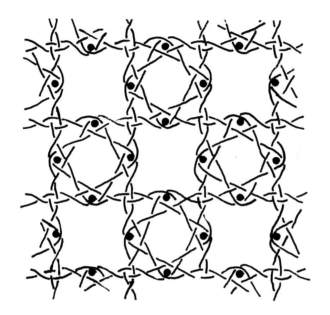

Scale Below is illustrated, in actual size, a strip of eighteenth-century Flemish lace, while on the next page the photograph is enlarged to the same scale as all the enlargements of all the stitches illustrated in the book. This should enable the reader to appreciate the relationship between the two when working the actual stitches.

The stitches illustrated in this piece of lace are as follows:
1 Half stitch ground
2 Twelve thread armure
3 Haloed spider
4 Toile star

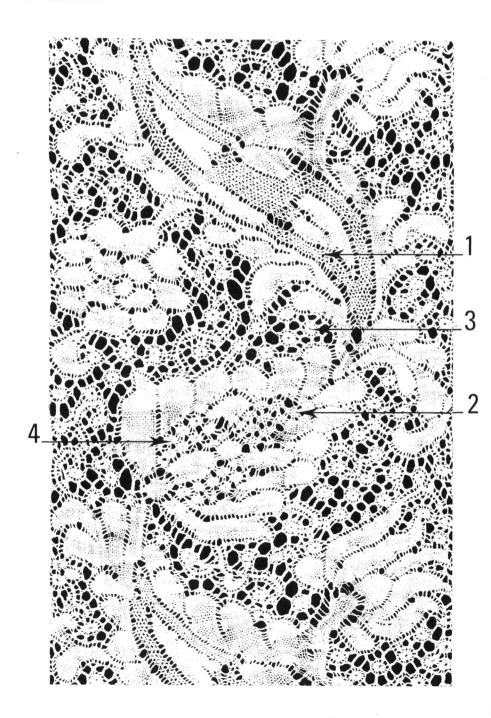

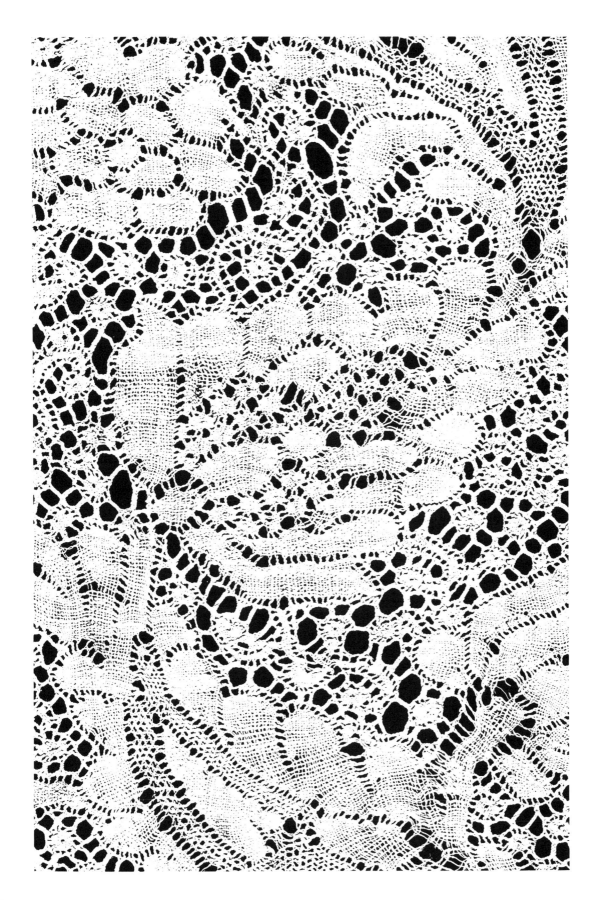

GLOSSARY

braid
A 4 thread plait made by continuous half stitches (fig. 1).

braid x
Number of half stitches per braid, e.g. braid x 3 means 3 half stitches, braid x 3½ means 3 half stitches plus a cross, so braid ends up untwisted.

1.

brick
1 pair weaving back and forth with winkie pins both sides. The worker of a brick always works over the first hole to the opposite hole, then weaves back and forth (fig. 2).

brides
Also called legs — connecting bars, either twisted or braided. Literal translation means 'bridges'.

2.

bud star
Star motif with centre filled diagonally (fig 3).

cross
Cross left hand thread over right hand thread.

diag.
Diagonal.

fish
With joint top and bottom having horizontal bars weaving through (fig. 4).

3.

h.s.
Half stitch, also called lattice stitch or gauze stitch: 2 over 3; 2 over 1; 4 over 3. Figures on diagram refer to positions only, not to the bobbins, therefore they must be recounted before each move (fig. 5).

honeycomb stitch
Half stitch, twist 1, pin, half stitch, twist 1 (fig. 6).

4.

horiz.
Horizontal.

1 2 3 4

lazy join
Also called a windmill; made with 4 pairs — each pair used as a single thread, make a wholestitch (fig. 7).

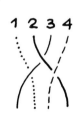

5.

6.

7.

leaf, leaves	Also called petals or wheat ears; usually start and finish with wholestitch to create the distinctive tight top and bottom (fig. 8).
legs	As brides — connecting bars, either twisted or braided.
lt hd rt hd	Left hand. Right hand.
no., nos	Number, numbers.
passives	Inactive pairs through which the worker passes.
pea	Cross between fish and spider with a pair worked in and out at centre, to complete the pattern (fig. 9).
picots — single	Make a loop by twisting the thread round a pin over and towards you (fig. 10).
picots — double	Left handed picots: tw. 3 left hand pair, pin pointing to left over left hand thread, bring thread round pin, next take right hand thread round the pin in clockwise motion, gently pull all the twists round pin, tw. 2 (fig. 11). Right handed picots: as above but reversed and pin *under* thread (fig. 12).
picots — knotted	(fig. 13).

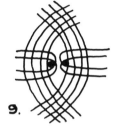

8.

9.

10.

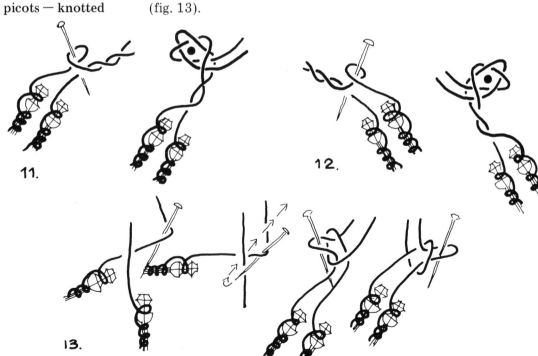

11.

12.

13.

pinchain	Using 2 pairs: half stitch, twist 1, pin, half stitch, twist 1 continuously along a single line (fig. 14).
pr, prs	Pair, pairs.
plait	Three threaded plait (fig. 15).

14.

raised tallies	Make an extra long leaf, pin, leave to one side, work pattern for underneath; with small stick, raise up leaf and remove pin from start and place between leaf pairs, replace pin in same hole.
ribbon	Usually a collection of untwisted passives making a decorative design.
rt hd	Right hand.
lt hd	Left hand.

15.

sewings	Joining one section to another by using a hook or needlepin to pull a loop through pinhole of worked side then threading the other bobbin of the worker pair through the loop (fig. 16).
sewings — double	Pull 2 loops through pinhole of worked side and thread the other 2 bobbins through loops.
shell star	Star motif with pairs entering and leaving to create a hole in the central area (fig. 17).
six thread cross	Cross centre 2 threads, pass top horizontal thread over and under twice, twist both diagonal pairs, then bottom horizontal thread under and over twice, twist middle 2 threads (fig. 18). This method can also be used in same manner to cross 6 pairs.
spiders	Wholestitch all left hand pairs through right hand pairs, pin, then wholestitch all right hand pairs through left hand pairs (fig. 19).

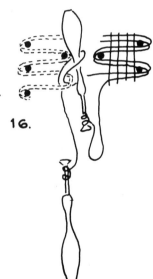

16.

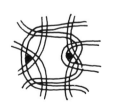

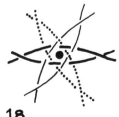

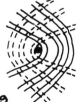

17.

18.

19.

stars	Divided into groups — toiles, shells, buds, and peas.
st.	Stitch.
tallies	Also called leadworks and cutworks (fig. 20).
toile star	Wholestitch star without pins (fig. 21).
tw.	Twist — right hand thread over left hand thread.
vert.	Vertical.
wholestitch block	1 pair weaving back and forth with winkie pins both sides; the worker always works *under* first right hand pin and ends on left hand side (fig. 22).
winkie pin	Decorative hole made by twisting worker pair round pin (usually twice) at side of work (fig. 23).
worker	The active pair — also called leaders or weavers.
w.s.	Wholestitch, also called cloth-stitch (fig. 24): 2 over 3; 2 over 1; 4 over 3; 2 over 3

Little dashes on prickings denote number of twists.

Empty circles denote temporary pins to be removed as soon as possible.

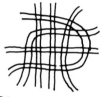

20.

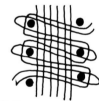

21.

22.

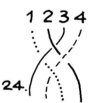

23.

1 2 3 4

24.

BOBBIN LACE STITCHES

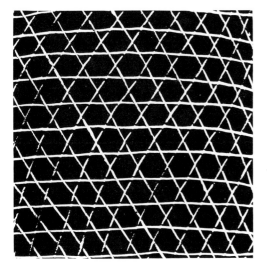

HALF STITCH GROUND

This stitch is also called Lattice stitch

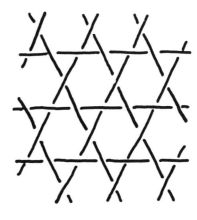

2 over 3, 2 over 1, 4 over 3

these figures refer to positions, not to the
   threads, therefore they must be
   recounted after each move

If you tw. 1 at edge pins the same thread
   weaves back and forth

if you tw. 2 at edge pins a new thread
   weaves each row

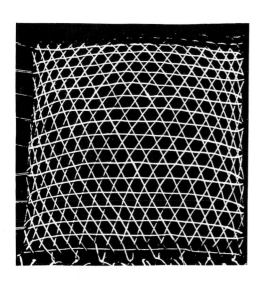

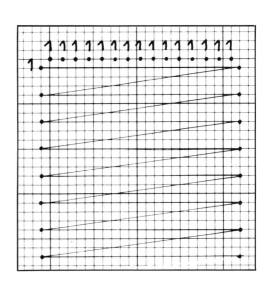

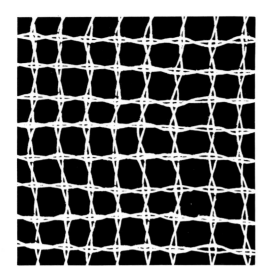

GAUZE GROUND

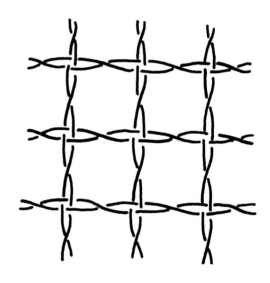

no pins
    except to hold horizontals to preserve
    true alignment

tw. 1, w.s., tw. 1, w.s.

for all horizontals and verticals

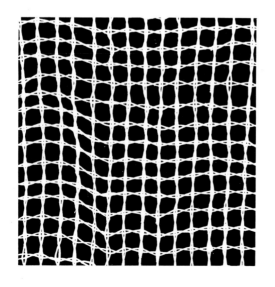

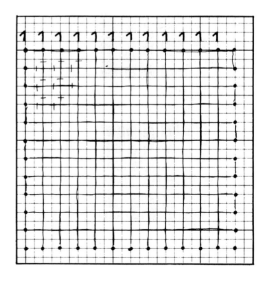

HALF GAUZE

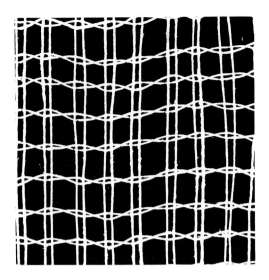

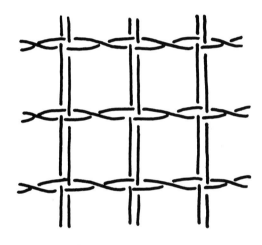

no pins
    except to hold horizontals to preserve
    alignment

tw. 1, w.s., tw. 1, w.s.

passives not twisted

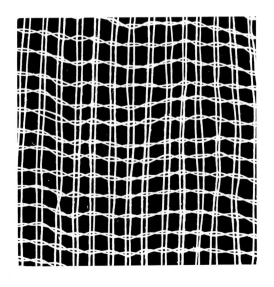

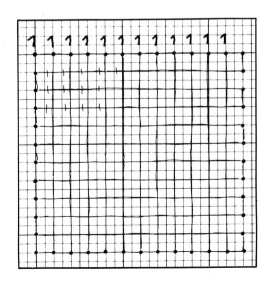

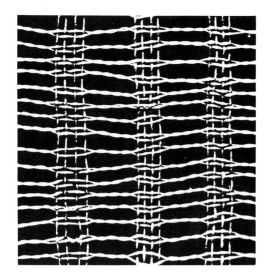

w.s., w.s., tw. 4, w.s., w.s.

no tw. on passives

pin to support only

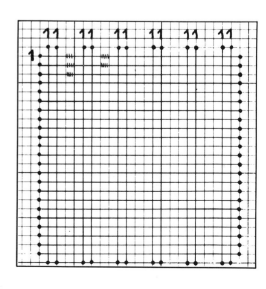

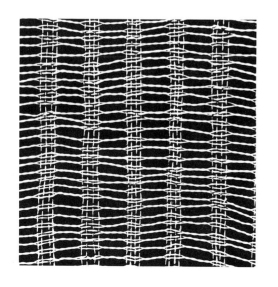

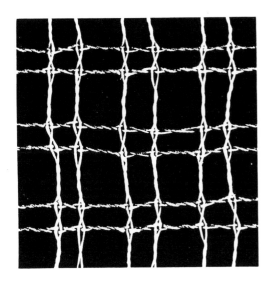

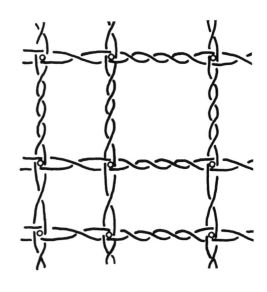

tw. 1 on short square

tw. 4 on long lines

w.s., with pin in middle at all joins

all pins removed after 2 rows, so as not
    to leave pinholes

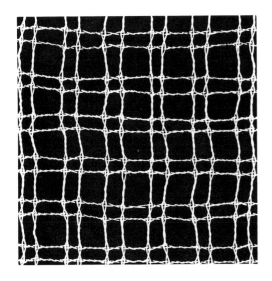

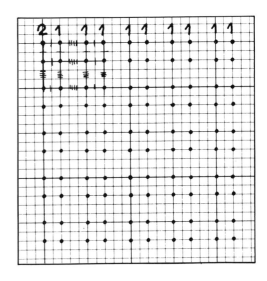

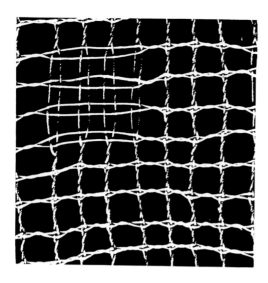

ITALIAN FILET WITH TOILE DOTS

w.s., tw. 2 workers and passives throughout
except untwisted w.s. squares
pin where necessary to retain shape

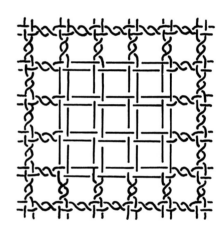

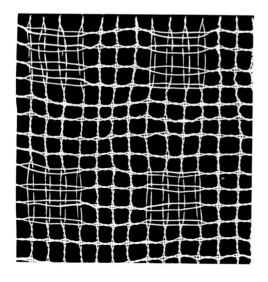

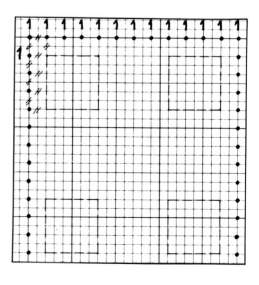

ABRUZZIAN POINT AND FLAT

This is so called after a province in Italy just east of Rome.

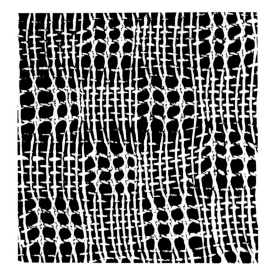

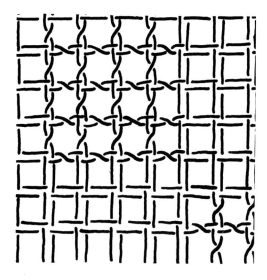

w.s., tw. 1 workers and passives x 4 for twisted squares

w.s. remainder

pin only where necessary to retain shape

note: there is an untwisted horizontal and vertical line between each square

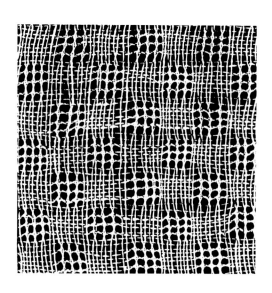

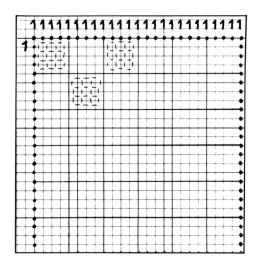

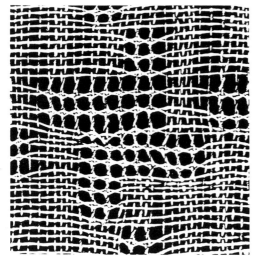

GAUZE SHAPES

tw. 1, w.s. workers and passives in open
  work

w.s. remainder

pin where necessary to retain shape

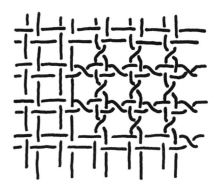

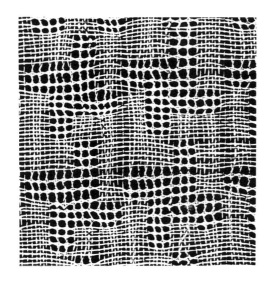

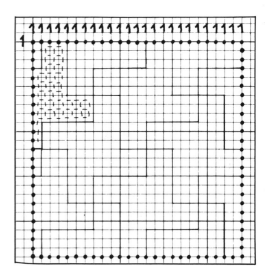

GARTER STITCH

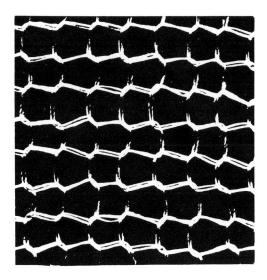

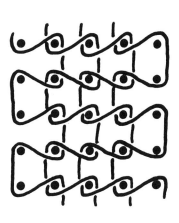

first row (left to right) lt over rt, pin,
   lt over rt

second row (right to left) rt over lt, pin,
   rt over lt

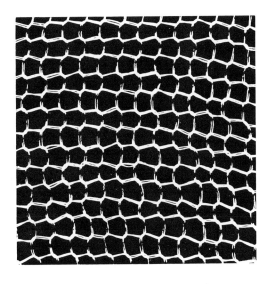

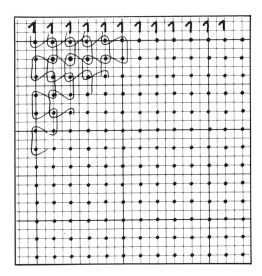

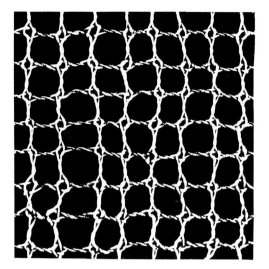

TULLE DOUBLE, DONE ON THE SQUARE

h.s., tw. 1, pin, h.s., tw. 1

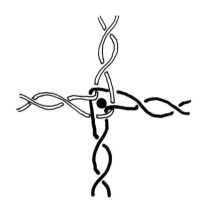

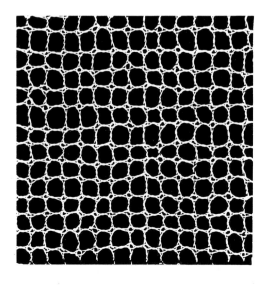

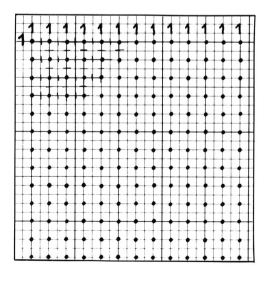

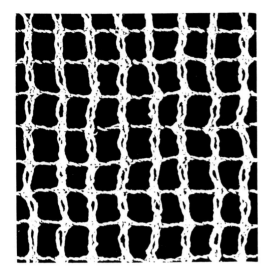

first work row of verticals:
    w.s., tw. 3, pin, w.s.

then work horizontal bar:
    w.s. through both vertical prs, tw. 3
    between each w.s. line to the end of
    row

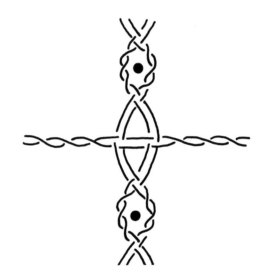

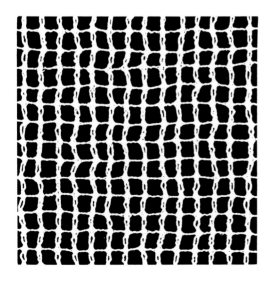

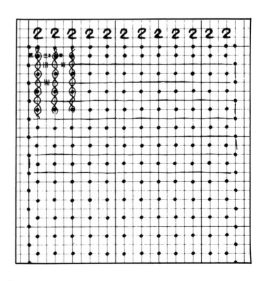

12

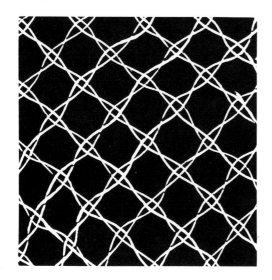

TORCHON GROUND

If made with extra twist between pins this is called Dieppe ground.

h.s., pin, h.s.

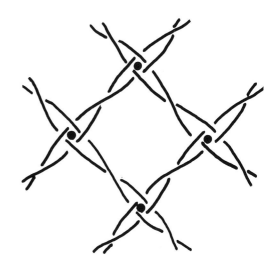

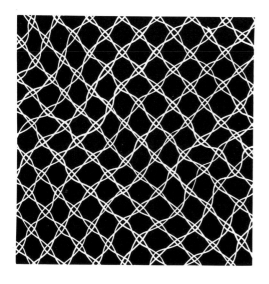

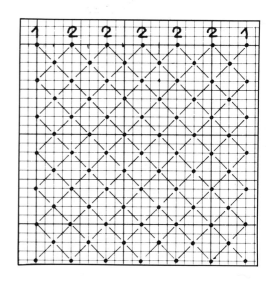

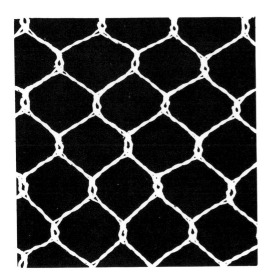

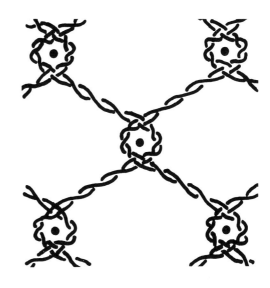

w.s., tw. 3

pin

w.s., tw. 3

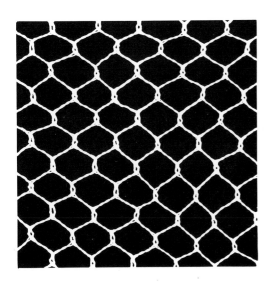

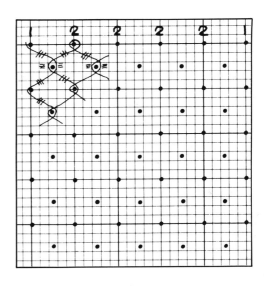

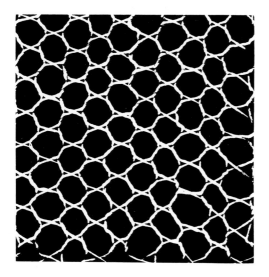

BUCKINGHAM POINT GROUND

This stitch, also called tulle or Lille ground, can be made with only one twist after each h.s. for a very fragile ground, or with three twists for a firm ground.

h.s., tw. 2, pin between the pairs

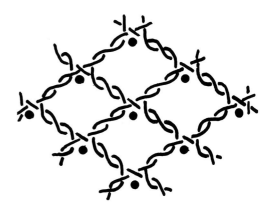

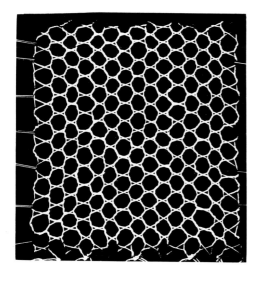

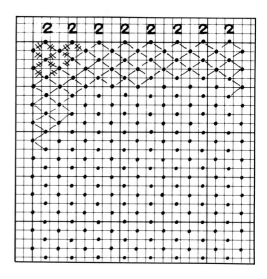

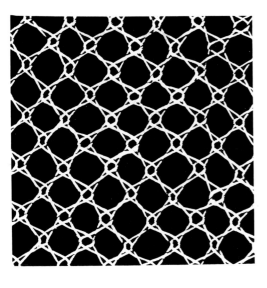

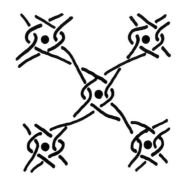

tw. 1 all legs to begin

h.s., tw. 1, pin, h.s. at each joint

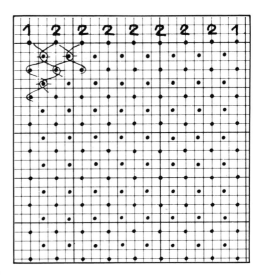

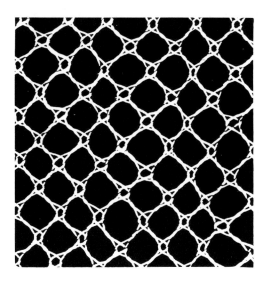

TWISTED HOLE GROUND WITH TWO TWISTS

tw. 2 all legs to begin

h.s., tw. 1, pin, h.s., tw. 1, at all joints

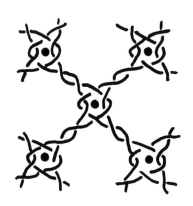

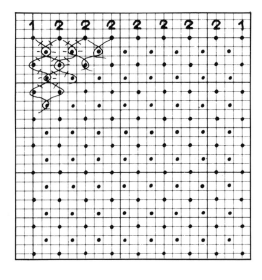

work continuous diagonal line first

then individual threads together in
  intermediate rows

tw. 1 rt hd thread over lt hd thread, pin,
  tw. 1 rt hd thread over lt hd thread at
  all pinholes

remove pins as soon as possible to leave
  no pinholes in final work

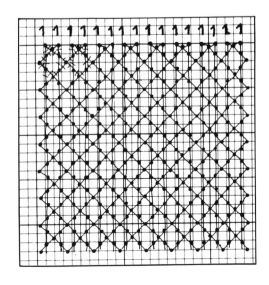

BRAIDED FLEMISH FILLING

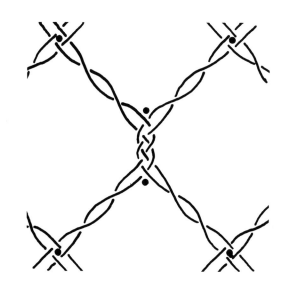

first and every alternate row: h.s., pin, h.s., tw. 1 both prs.

second row etc: pin, braid x 4 against pin, pin bottom of braid to hold, tw. 1 both prs

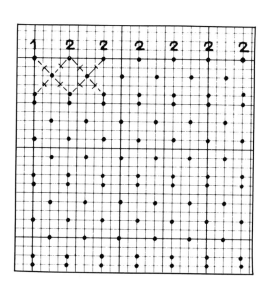

This stitch can also be made with five braids between pins.

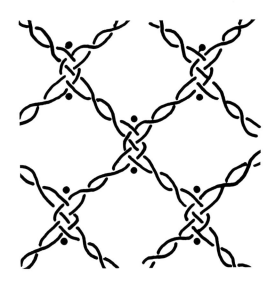

pin

braid x 3 hard against pin

pin

divide legs tw. 1

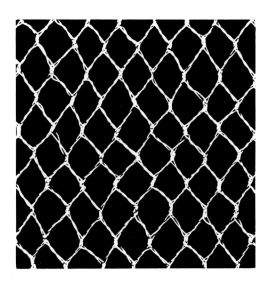

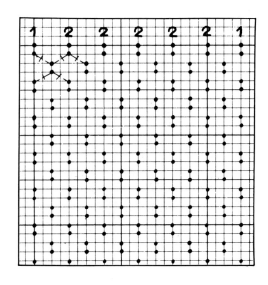

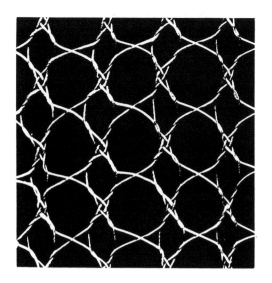

TORCHON AND HALF STITCH GROUND

first row and every alternate row:
   h.s., pin, h.s., tw. 1

second row etc:
   h.s., pin, tw. 1

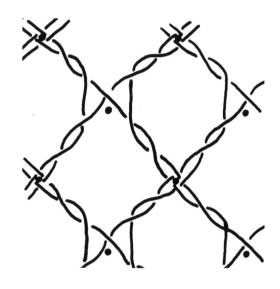

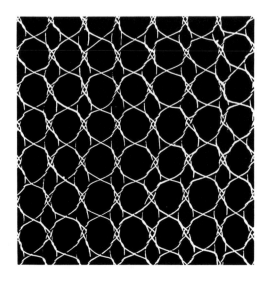

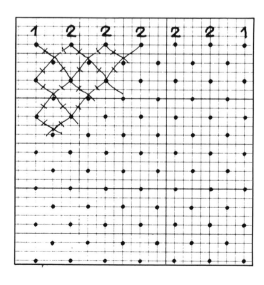

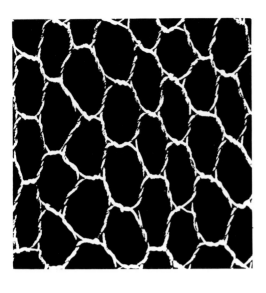

LILLE WORKED SIDEWAYS

tw. 3 vert. prs

with 1 lt hd bobbin wind round x 3 rt
    hd thread of lt hd pr

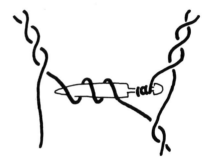

pull bobbin through loops created and this
    bobbin now becomes one of the lt hd
    pr and the lt hd bobbin ends on the
    right

in fact a triple reef knot has been made,
    and the bobbins have changed sides

pin only to keep shape

note: not an easy filling to keep neat

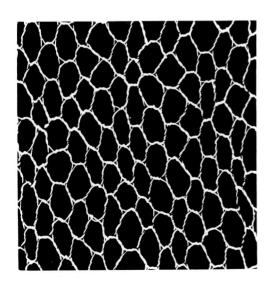

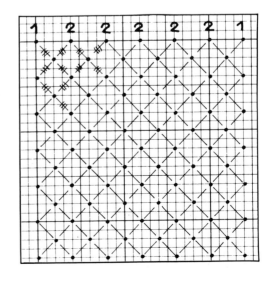

TULLE DU PUY

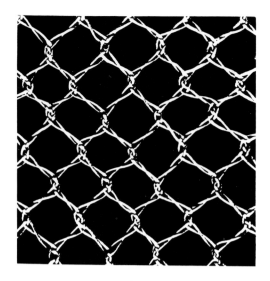

diagonals: tw. 1

joints: w.s., pin, w.s.

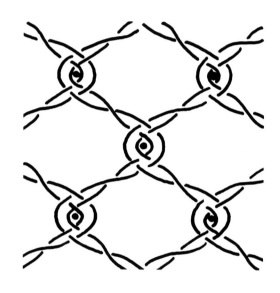

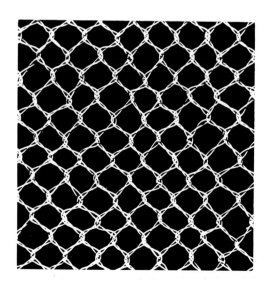

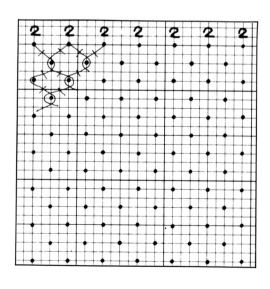

TORCHON DOUBLE GROUND

Torchon double ground can also be made with three twists to give a more open effect.

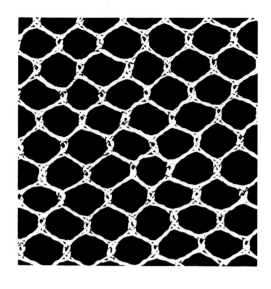

tw. 2 diagonals to start

w.s., tw. 1, pin, w.s., tw. 2

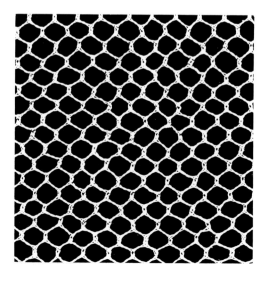

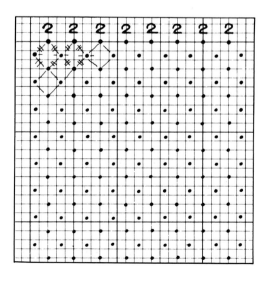

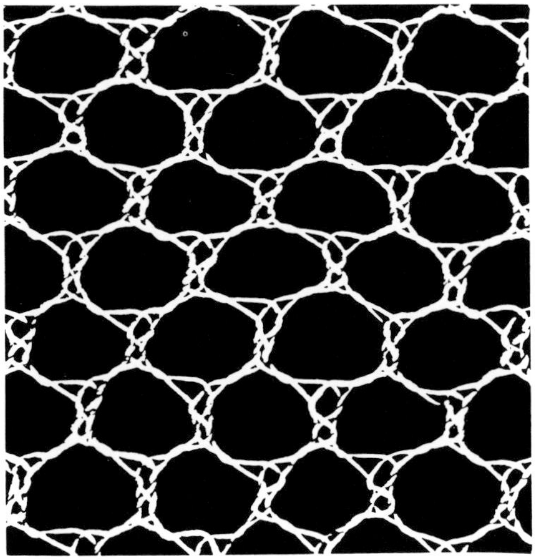

TRIPLE HALF STITCH GROUND

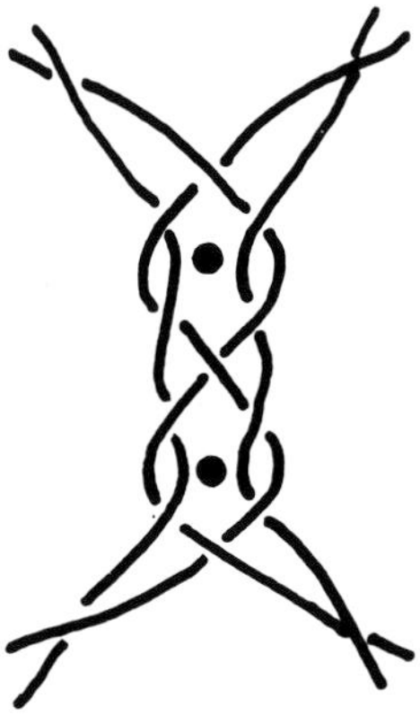

tw. 2 all legs to begin

h.s., pin, tw. 1, h.s., pin, tw. 1, h.s., tw. 1 at each joint

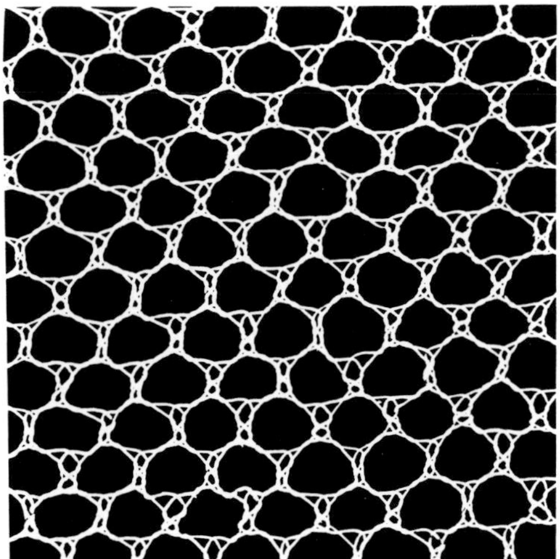

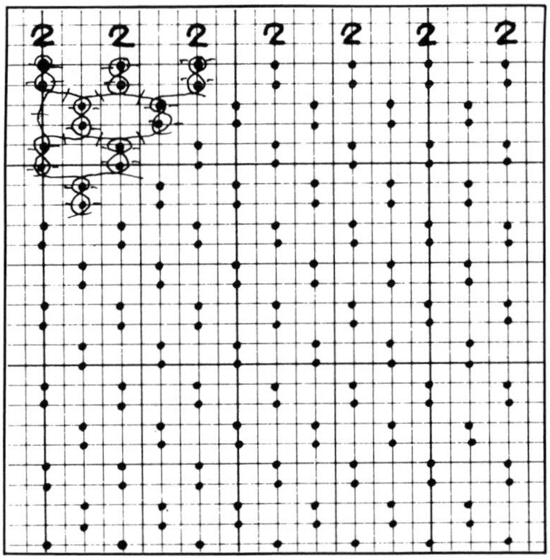

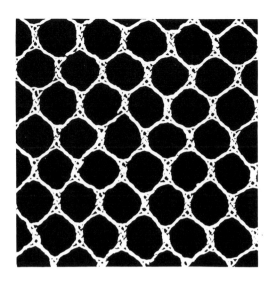

braid x 4

tw. 2 both prs at bottom of braids

divide prs and with pr from adjacent braid
make braid of next row

should be made with no pins, but when a
large area is to be filled it is best to
use temporary pins at top and bottom
of braids and remove pins as soon as
possible

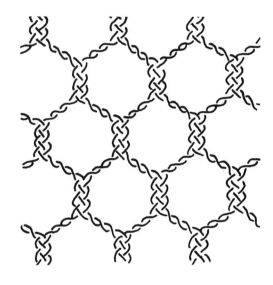

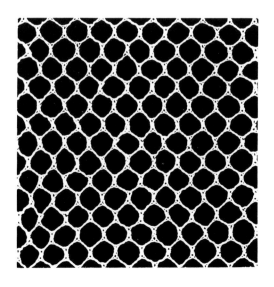

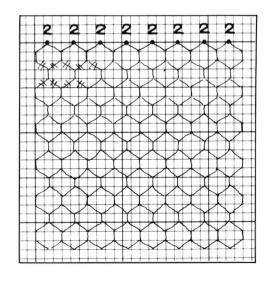

BRUSSELS NET

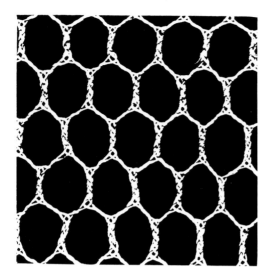

braid x 6

tw. 2 both prs at bottom of braids

divide prs and with pr from adjacent
  braid make braid of next row

should be made with no pins, but when a
  large area is to be filled it is best to use
  temporary pins at top and bottom of
  braids and remove pins as soon as
  possible

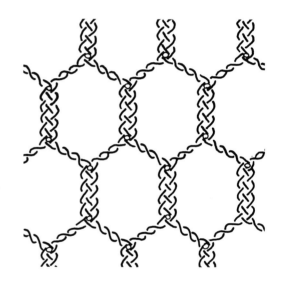

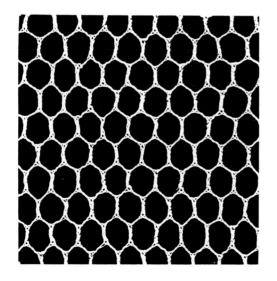

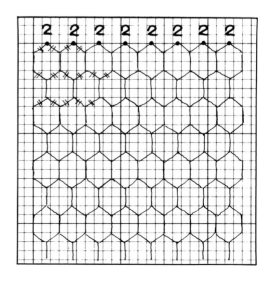

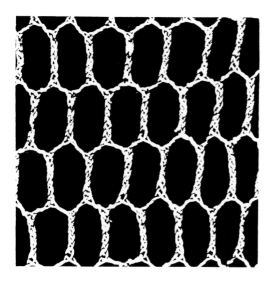

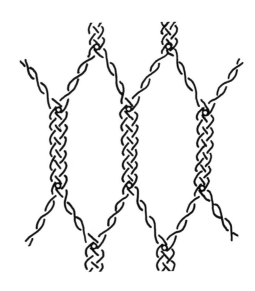

braid x 8

tw. 2 both prs at bottom of braids

divide prs and with pr from adjacent braid
  make braid of next row

should be made with no pins, but when
  a large area is to be filled it is best to
  use temporary pins at top and bottom
  of braids and remove pins as soon as
  possible

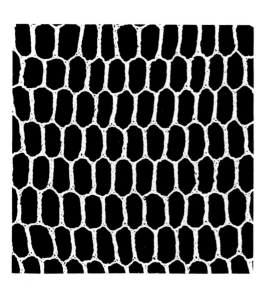

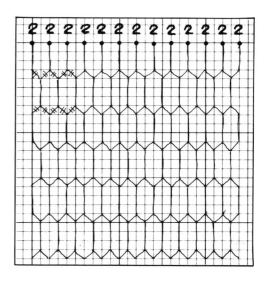

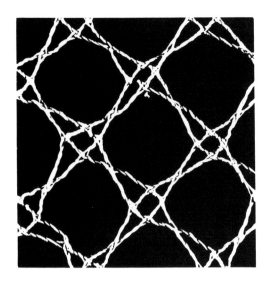

DEVONSHIRE
DOUBLE GROUND

tw. 3 between w.s. joints

support pins only

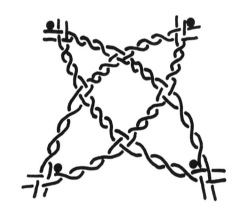

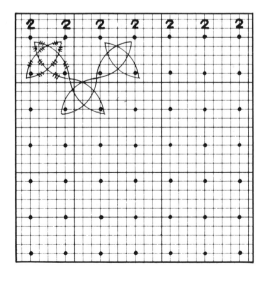

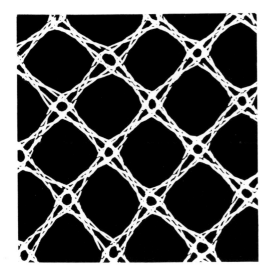

CANE GROUND

This can also be made with three twists
throughout: four pins are then needed
in the corners of the squares to support it.

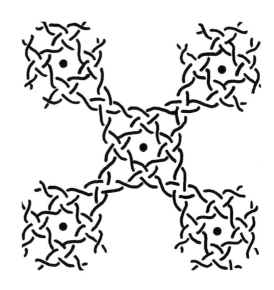

w.s., tw. 1 throughout

put pin in centre hole only

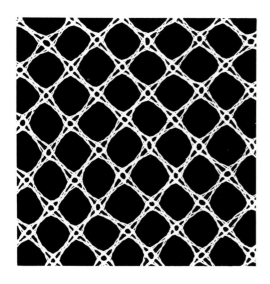

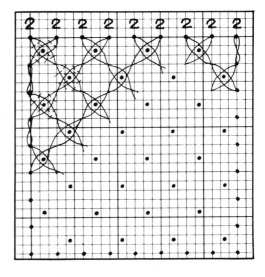

DIAGONAL PLAID 1

tw. 2 each pair between w.s. joints

pin base of joint to support

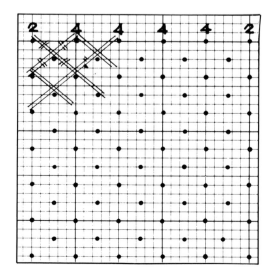

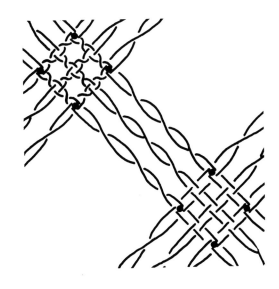

first row of diamonds:
w.s., tw. 1, w.s., tw. 1, w.s.

tw. 3 all diagonals between diamonds

next row of diamonds:
   w.s. x 3

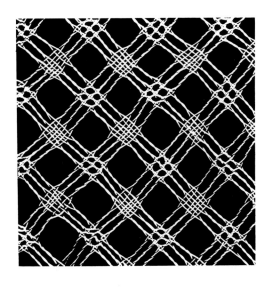

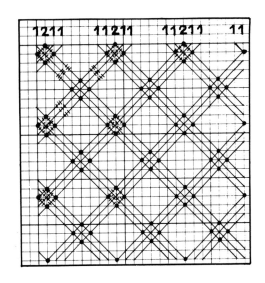

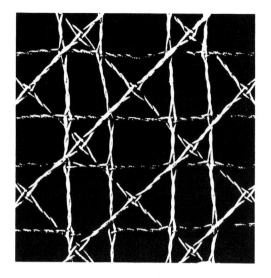

SQUARE MESH WITH 3D EFFECT

hollow lines — under
dotted lines — over

verticals and horizontals:

tw. 4 on sides of large squares

tw. 2 on sides of small squares

w.s. where they meet

diagonals:

tw. 4, w.s. pin to hold

lt hd diagonals placed *under* verticals
and horizontals

rt hd diagonals placed *over* verticals and
horizontals

all pins removed after 2 rows so as not
to leave pinholes

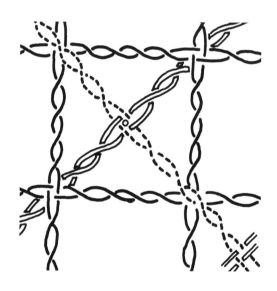

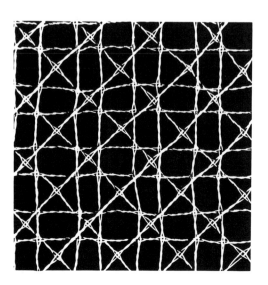

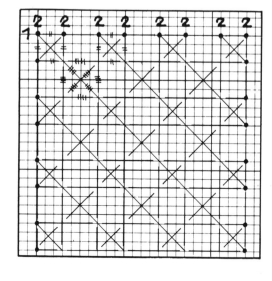

LAYERED GAUZE

diagonals w.s. through each other

horizontal pr: tw. 3 then one thread on
    top of the other below w.s. of diagonals,
    tw. 3 to end of row

work horizontals lt to rt one row, and
    rt to lt next row

pin only where necessary to retain shape

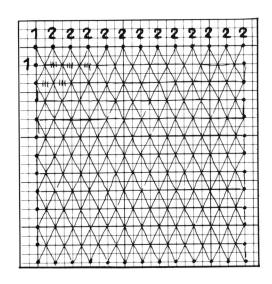

STAR AND LAYERED GAUZE

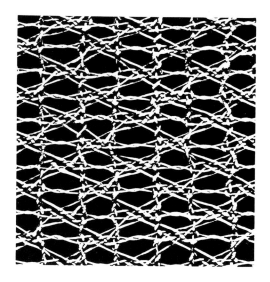

where diagonals pass through verticals:
    tw. 1 vert., lay both threads of diag.
    between and tw. 1 again

w.s. where horiz. and vert. meet

no tw. 1 on diag.

tw. 2 horiz. between stars

six thread cross: cross centre 2 threads,
    pass top horiz. thread over and under
    twice, twist both diag. prs, then bottom
    horiz. thread under and over twice,
    twist middle 2 threads

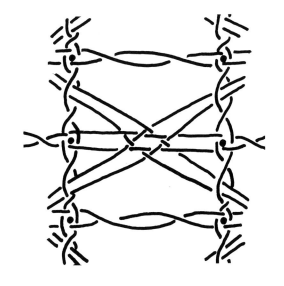

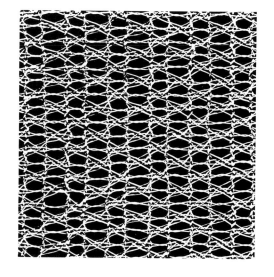

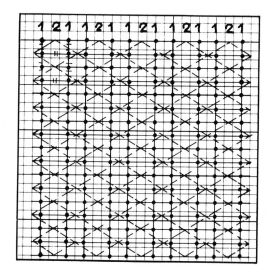

COBWEB

Cobweb stitch is also sometimes called
Boule de Neige or Fausse Valenciennes.

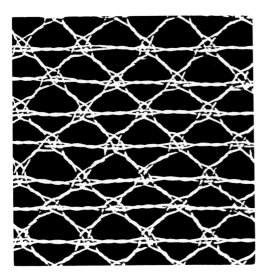

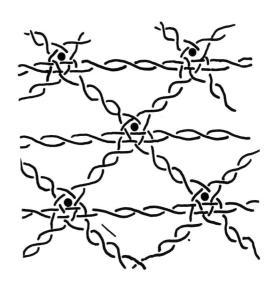

tw. 3 to start all diagonals

h.s., pin each set of 2 diag. prs

w.s. horizontal bar through these prs,
   tw. 3

work horizontal bar lt to rt one row, and
   rt to lt next row

h.s., tw. 2 diagonal prs

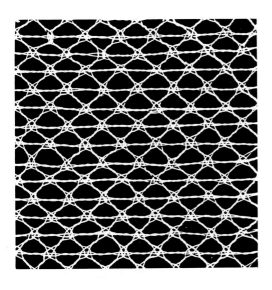

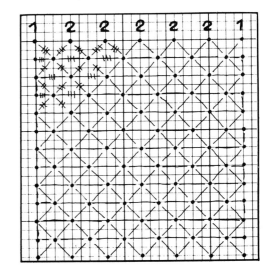

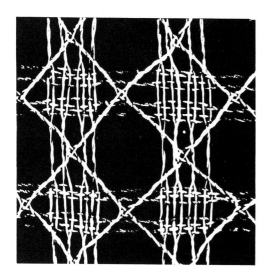

PLAID

(1) w.s. through 4 passives tw. 4 lifting diagonals and working under them

(2) w.s. x 4, tw. 1, slip one thread diag. through tw. 2, slip other diag. through, tw. 1, w.s. x 4

both diagonals tw. 1, w.s., pin, tw. 1

(3) as (2)

(4) as (1)

(5) work diagonals over verticals tw. 4

(6) tw. 1 verticals, thread diag. through, tw. 2, thread other diag. through, tw. 1

diagonals tw. 1, w.s., tw. 1

(7) as (6)

(8) as (5)

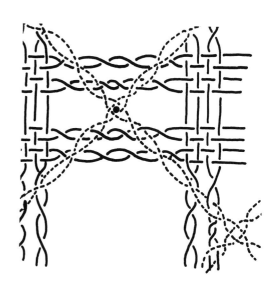

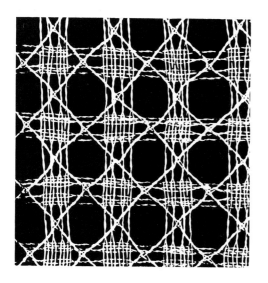

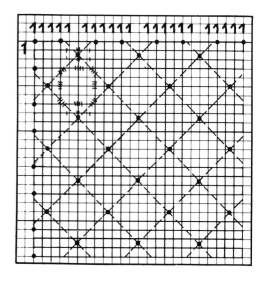

UNTWISTED KAT STITCH

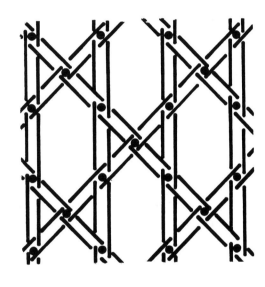

no twists throughout

w.s. with pin in middle

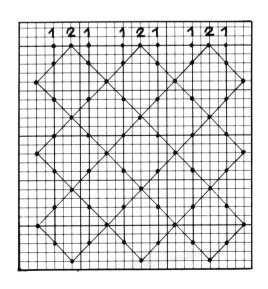

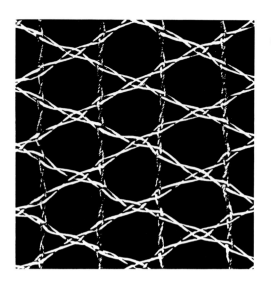

KAT STITCH

Kat stitch is also sometimes called star mesh or double ground.

1 tw. between each joint

joint: w.s. with pin in middle

remove pins after 2 rows so as not to leave pinholes

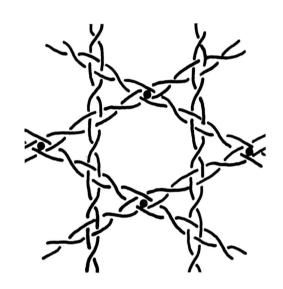

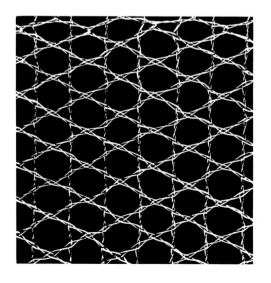

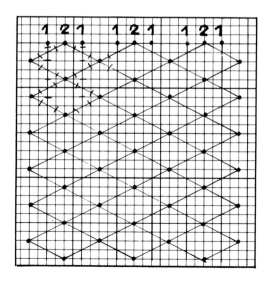

POINT DU MARIAGE

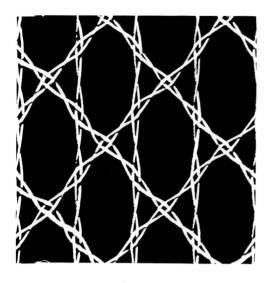

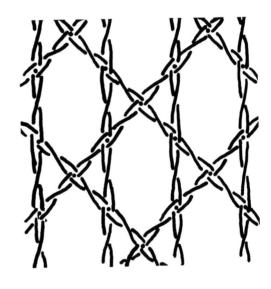

1 tw. between each joint

h.s., pin, h.s.

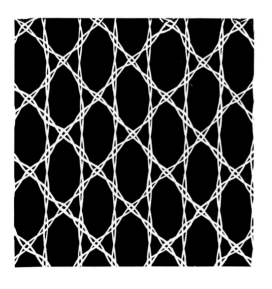

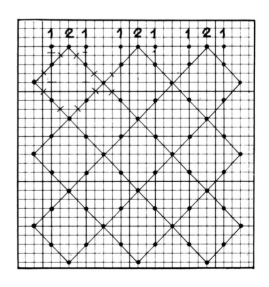

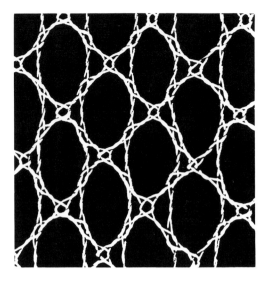

SCANDINAVIAN GROUND 1

h.s., tw. 1, pin, h.s., tw. 1 at each pinhole

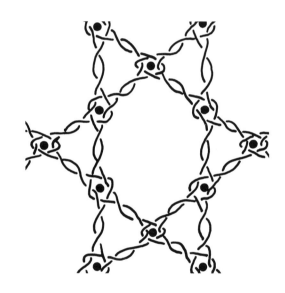

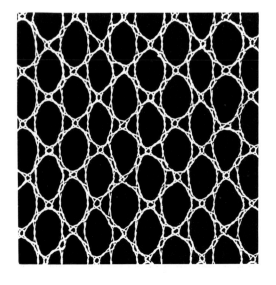

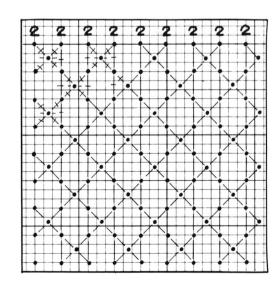

SCANDINAVIAN GROUND 2

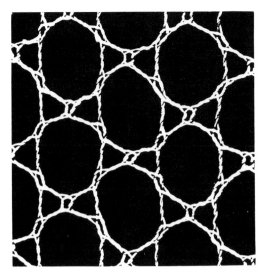

h.s., tw. 2, pin, h.s., tw. 2 at each pinhole

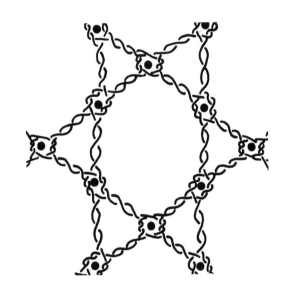

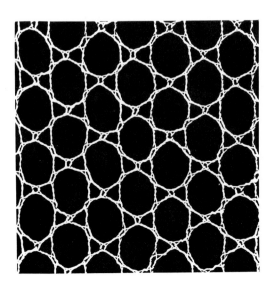

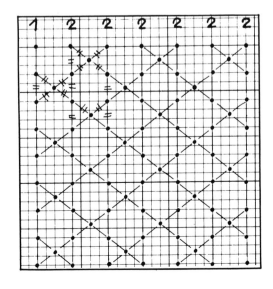

HONEYCOMB NET

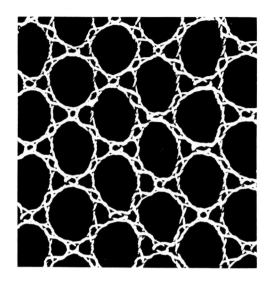

h.s., tw. 1, pin, h.s., tw. 1 (honeycomb
stitch) at every pinhole

work continuous diag. line first

then intermediate rows, honeycomb
stitch individual prs together

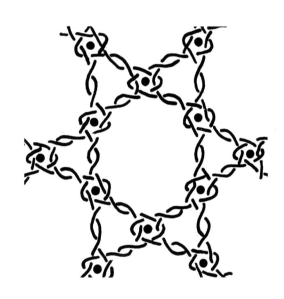

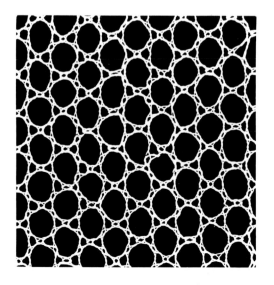

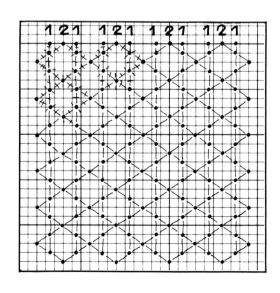

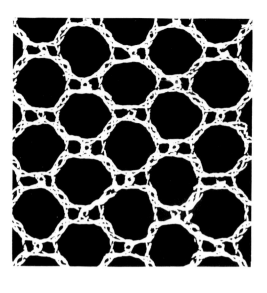

WHOLESTITCH HONEYCOMB

w.s., tw. 1, pin, w.s., tw. 1 at each pinhole

work continuous diag. line first

then intermediate row:
    individual prs together

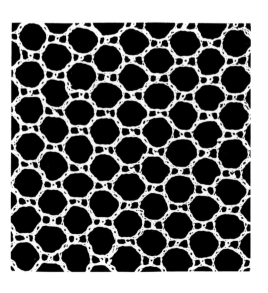

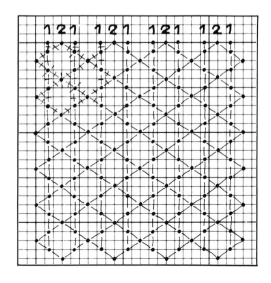

BRAID AND LOCK STITCH

braid each leg

tw. 3 inside prs

with corresponding pr from adjacent
    braid: w.s., tw. 1, pin, w.s., tw. 3

tw. 1 outside pr

braid to next lock stitch

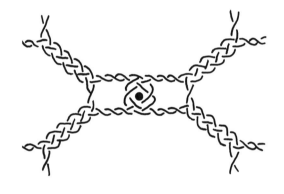

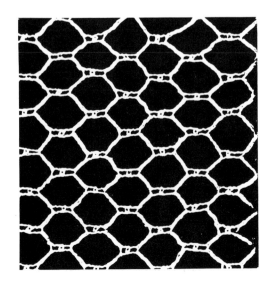

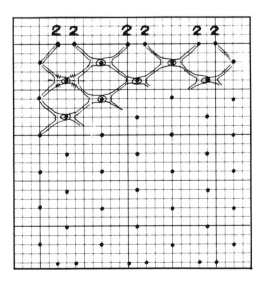

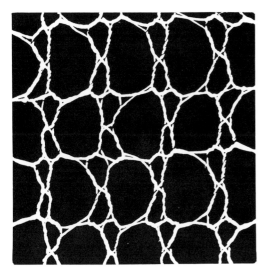

DEVONSHIRE
HONEYCOMB FILLING

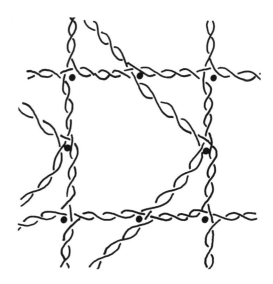

h.s., tw. 3 at each pinhole

horizontal line weaves back and forth
every alternate row

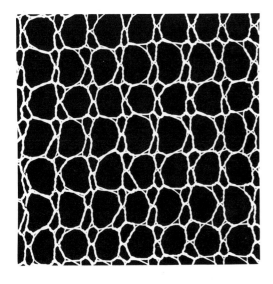

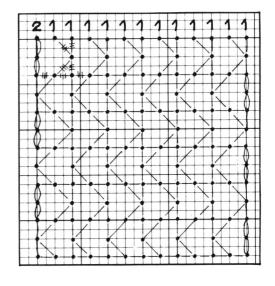

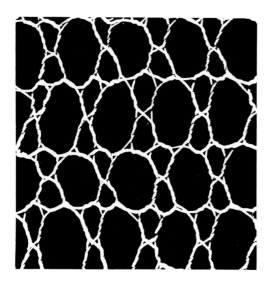

DEVONSHIRE HONEYCOMB VARIATION

h.s., tw. 3 at each pinhole

horizontal line weaves back and forth
every alternate row

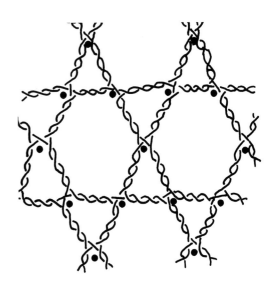

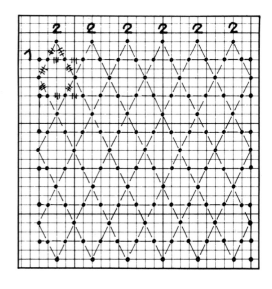

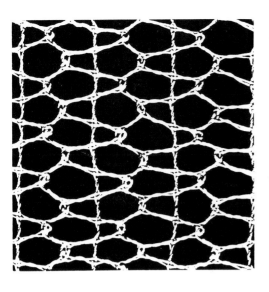

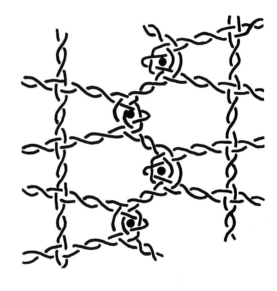

w.s., pin, tw. 2 worker only

w.s., tw. 2 when worker meets zigzag
   passive

w.s., tw. 2 elsewhere

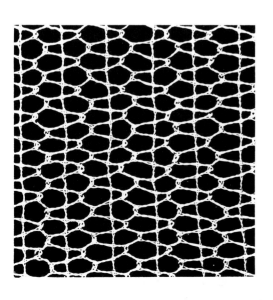

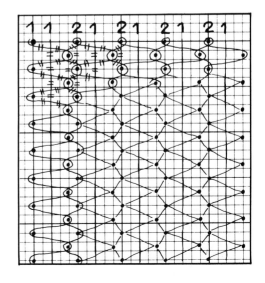

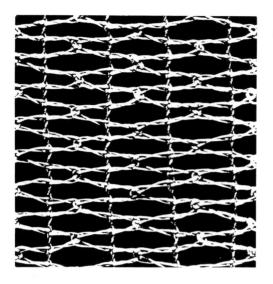

LOCK STITCH

This is a Du Puy De Paris variation,
otherwise known as Torchon Mode.

w.s., pin, w.s.

one tw. between each stitch

w.s. at each joint

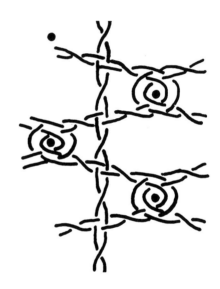

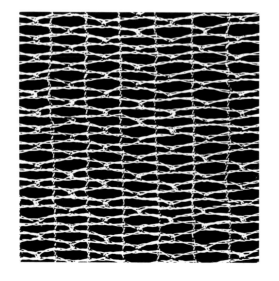

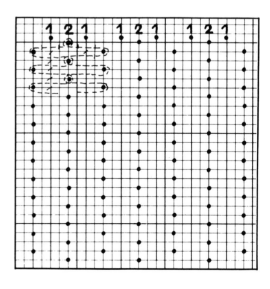

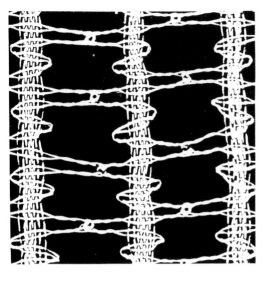

LOCK STITCH AND
WINKIE PIN

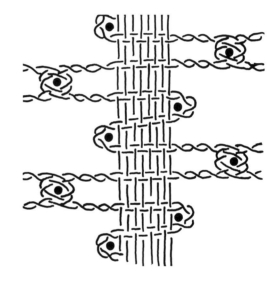

lock stitch: tw. 3, w.s. with adjacent pr,
   tw. 1, pin, w.s. back, tw. 3

w.s. through 4 passives

tw. 3 around winkie pins

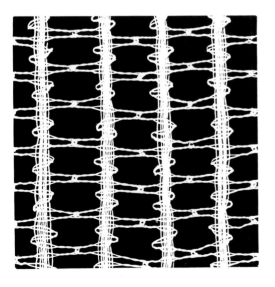

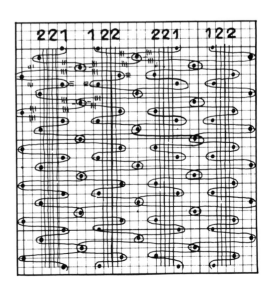

221 122 221 122

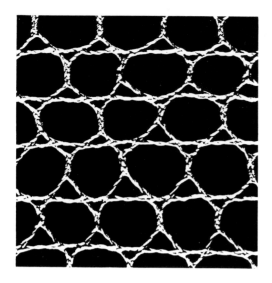

POINT DE PARIS VARIATION WITH BRAIDED SIDES

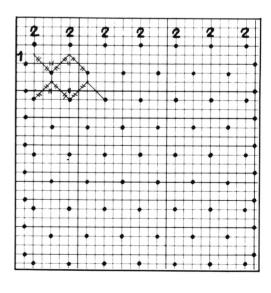

tw. 2 and w.s. all joints of diagonals and
horizontals

pin before braid

braid 4 times hard against the pin

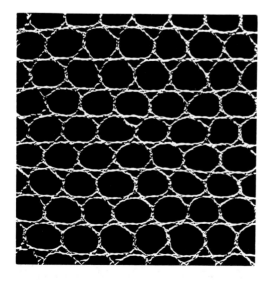

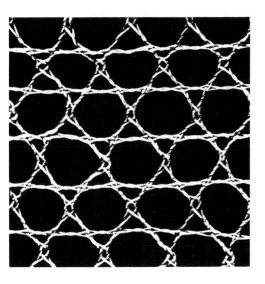

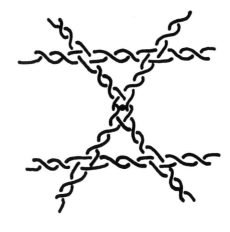

tw. 2 between all joints

w.s. where horiz. and diag. lines cross

h.s., tw. 1, pin, h.s., tw. 1 where 2 diag.
    lines cross

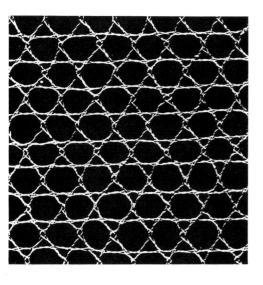

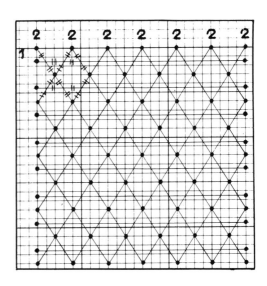

THREE THREADED POINT DE PARIS

work horizontally only

when working left to right:
  (1) h.s. with next pr to right
  (2) pin between lt hd pr, tw. 2 lt hd
      pr and leave
  (3) tw. 2 rt hd pr, repeat from (1) to
      end of row

when working right to left:
  (1) h.s. with next pr to left
  (2) pin between rt hd pr., tw. 2 rt hd pr
  (3) tw. 2 lt hd pr, repeat from (1) to
      end of row

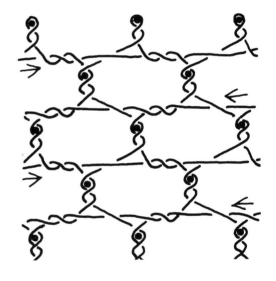

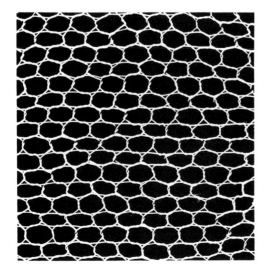

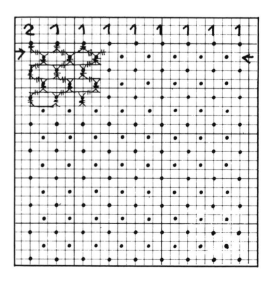

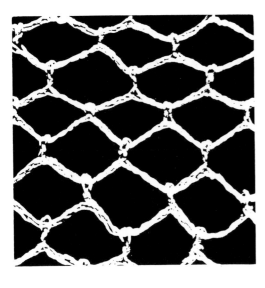

SIX SIDED BOBBIN MESH

braid x 10½

sew top pr over middle of loop above,
    pin, gently pull threads to correct
    distance between loops, then sew round
    this newly formed loop

note: very difficult to keep tidy

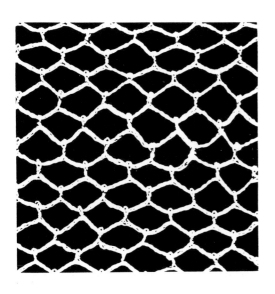

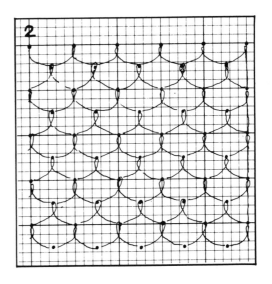

FEATHER GROUND

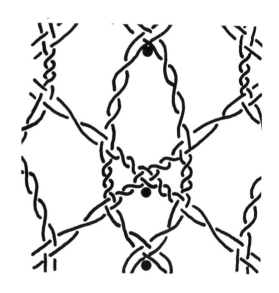

all joints are w.s.

supporting pins are placed under crossings

tw. 2 within feather

tw. 1 diagonals outside feather

feather: tw. 3 top two sections and tw. 1
    bottom section

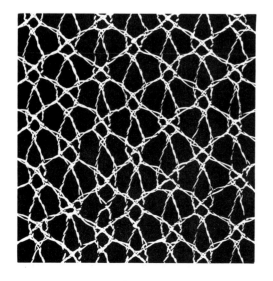

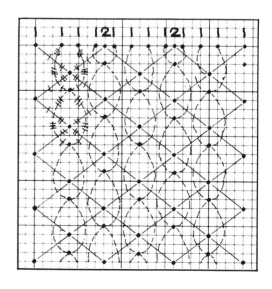

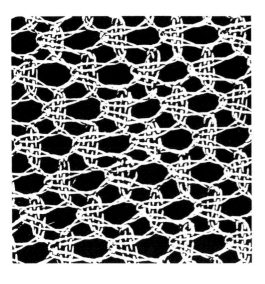

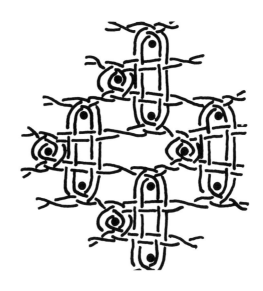

w.s. throughout

pin to support top and bottom of lozenge

w.s., pin, w.s. at apex of triangle

tw. 1 between triangles

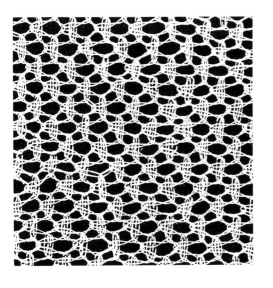

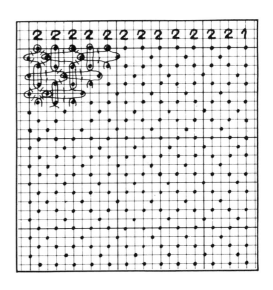

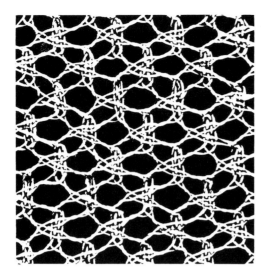

TRIANGULAR GROUND 2

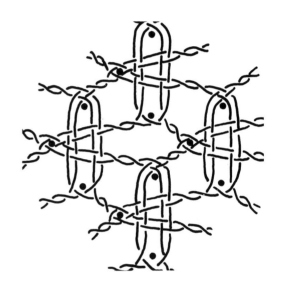

tw. 2 before top of lozenge

w.s. throughout triangle

pin top and bottom of lozenge

w.s. with pin in middle at apex of triangle

h.s., tw. 1 at bottom of lozenge

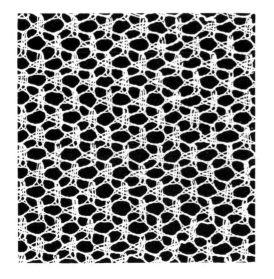

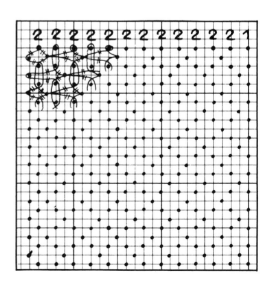

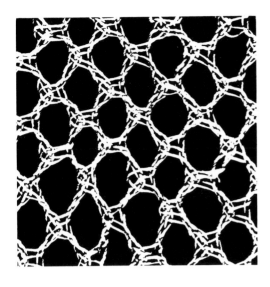

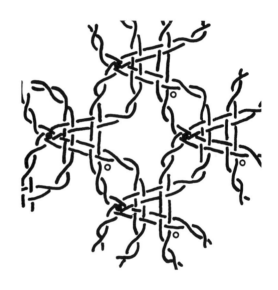

w.s. throughout

w.s. with pin in middle at apex of triangle

tw. 2 between triangles

pin only to keep shape between rt hd
   prs at bottom of triangle

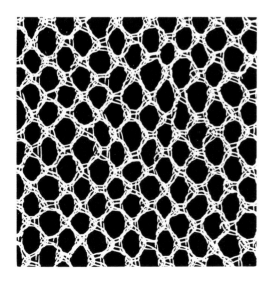

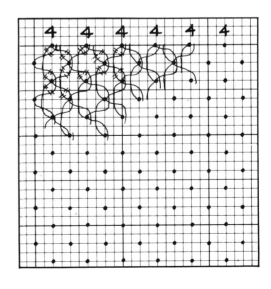

TRIANGULAR GROUND 4

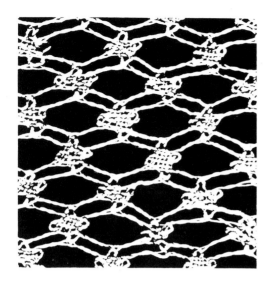

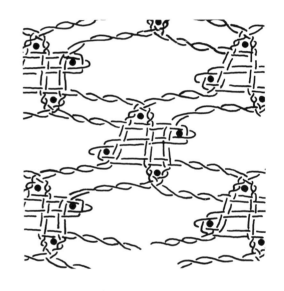

made in 4 pin groups

tw. 3 all 4 legs

w.s., pin centre 2 prs, tw. 2

w.s. 2nd lt hd leg back and forth through the 3 prs, tw. 2 at winkie pins, ending on rt hd side

tw. 2 centre 2 prs and w.s. through each other

tw. 3 all 4 legs

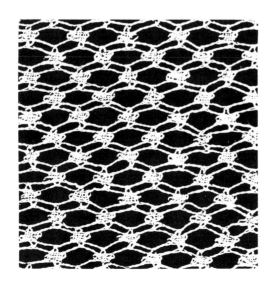

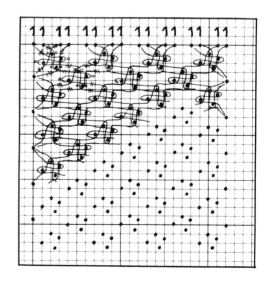

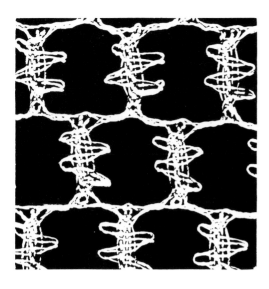

at top of block: w.s., tw. 3 2 centre prs, pin, w.s.

w.s. 2 lt hd prs and 2 rt hd prs

3rd pr from lt becomes worker, w.s. to lt through 2 prs

work back and forth through 3 prs with tw. 3 round winkie pins, ending on lt hd side

w.s. 2 rt hd prs

w.s. 2 centre prs, tw. 3, pin, w.s.

tw. 1, h.s. x 3 to next block

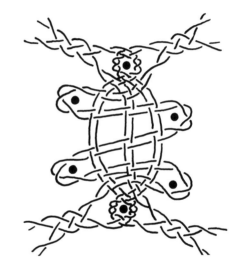

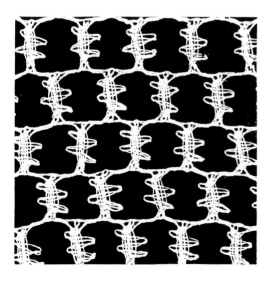

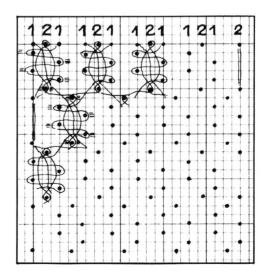

BIAS GROUND 1

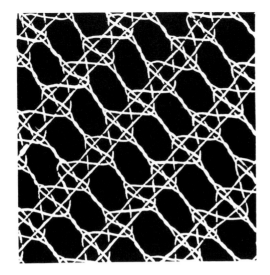

3, 4, 5, 6 = 4 pin block

$$4 \quad \begin{array}{c} 1 \ 3 \ 2 \\ \diamondsuit \\ 7 \ 6 \ 8 \end{array} \quad 5$$

1, 2, 7, 8 = intervening stitches

work on diagonal only

4 pin block: h.s., pin, h.s. at 3, 5, 4 and
    6, but work h.s. 2 middle prs between
    the pins numbered 4 and 5

h.s. 2 lt hd prs between blocks

tw. 3 each pr between rows

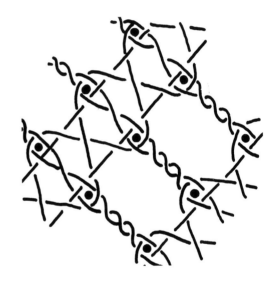

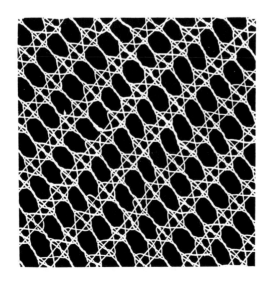

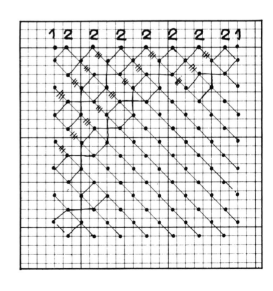

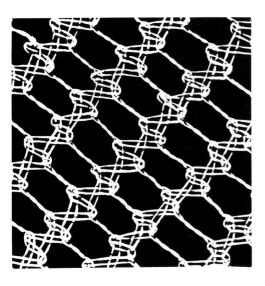

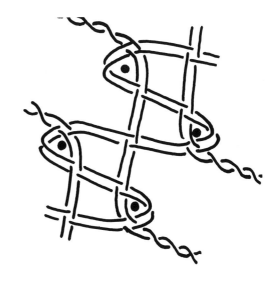

work on the diagonal only

w.s., tw. 1 worker pr, pin, w.s.

w.s. through passives

tw. 3 between rows

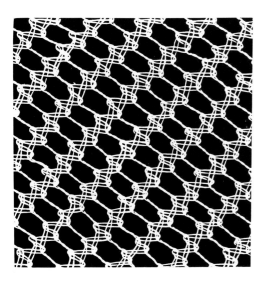

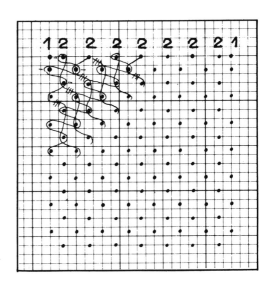

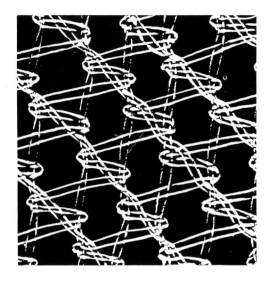

BIAS GROUND 3

w.s. throughout

no twisting of passives or weaver except
   at pinholes

at pinholes tw. 3

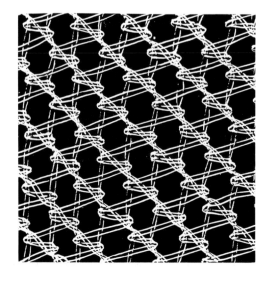

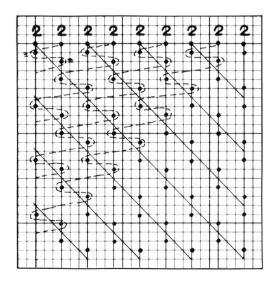

BIAS GROUND 4

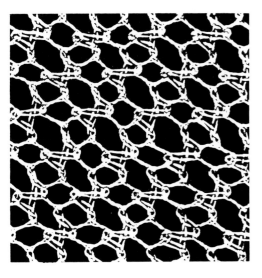

rt hd leg becomes the worker pr

w.s. back and forth picking up a leg to the
   rt and lt, then leave out legs until
   original 2 prs

tw. 1 workers at winkie pin

tw. 2 between diamonds

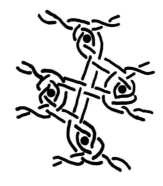

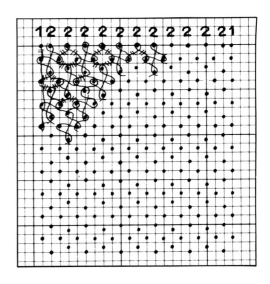

BIAS GROUND 5

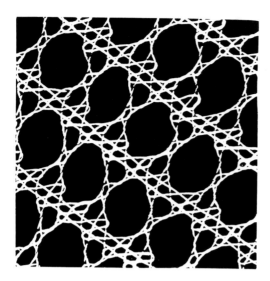

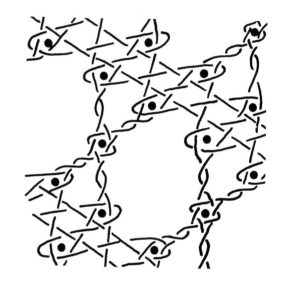

h.s. back and forth down diagonals, picking
  up prs on rt hd side and leaving out
  prs on lt hd side; tw. 1 round pins at
  sides

tw. 1 all prs before crosses

h.s., tw. 1, pin, h.s., tw. 1 at pinholes
  between diagonals

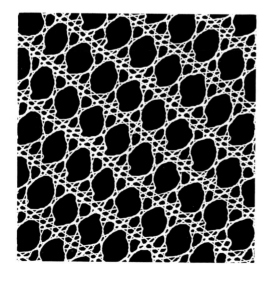

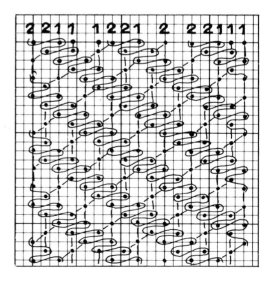

ROSE GROUND 1

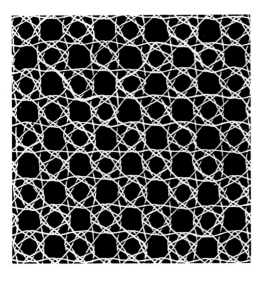

3, 4, 5, 6 = 4 pin block

```
      1 3 2
   4  ◇  5
      7 6 8
```

1, 2, 7, 8 = intervening stitches

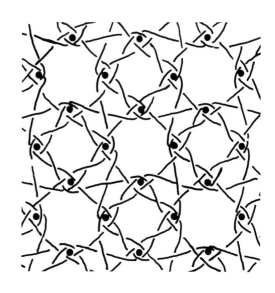

4 pin block: h.s., pin, h.s.

intervening stitches: h.s. with no pin

next row as above but omitting top h.s.

spaces and blocks alternated each row

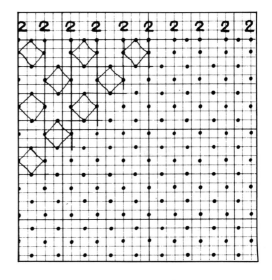

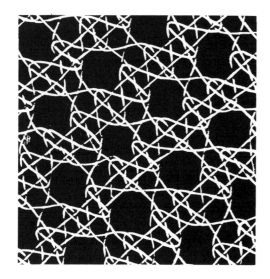

ROSE GROUND 2

3, 4, 5, 6 = 4 pin block

```
      1 3 2
   4  ◇  5
      7 6 8
```

1, 2, 7, 8 = intervening stitches

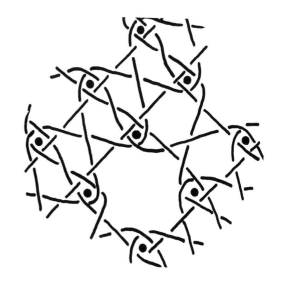

worked on diagonal only

4 pin block: h.s., pin, h.s.

work in this sequence
    pinhole 3
    pinhole 5
    work h.s. 2 middle prs between 4 & 5
    pinhole 4
    pinhole 6

intervening stitches:
    h.s.

blocks and spaces alternate each row

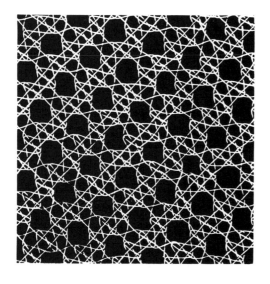

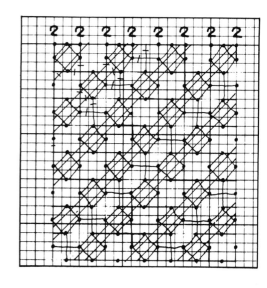

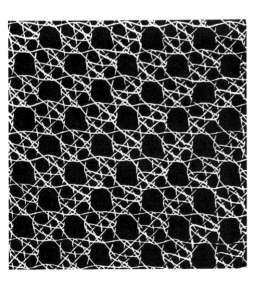

3, 4, 5, 6 = 4 pin block

```
    1 3 2
 4  ◇  5
    7 6 8
```

1, 2, 7, 8 = intervening stitches

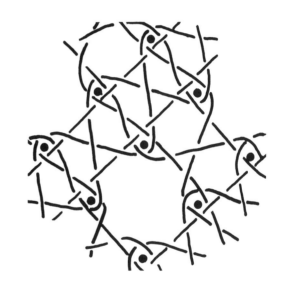

4 pin block: h.s., pin, h.s.

work in this sequence
    pinhole 3
    pinhole 5

work h.s. 2 middle prs
    between 4 & 5
    pinhole 4
    pinhole 6

intervening stitches: h.s.

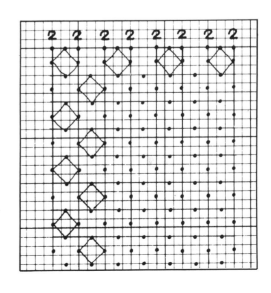

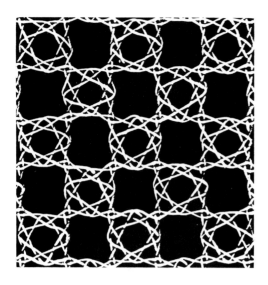

ROSE GROUND 4

3, 4, 5, 6 = 4 pin block

```
    1 3 2
  4  ◇  5
    7 6 8
```

1, 2, 7, 8 = intervening stitches

4 pin block: h.s., pin, h.s.

intervening stitches: w.s., tw. 1 (no pin)

spaces and blocks alternated each row

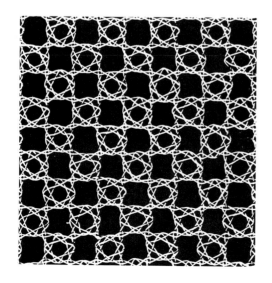

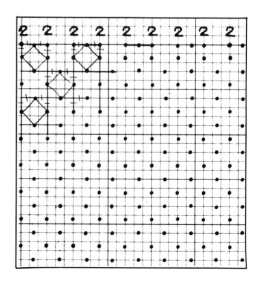

ROSE GROUND 5

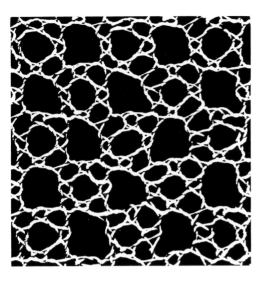

3, 4, 5, 6 = 4 pin block

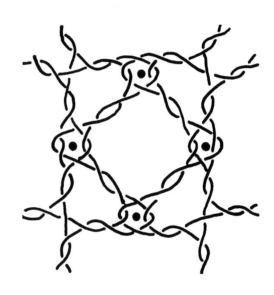

1, 2, 7, 8 = intervening stitches

4 pin block: h.s., tw. 1, pin, h.s., tw. 1

intervening stitches: h.s., tw. 1

spaces and blocks alternated each row

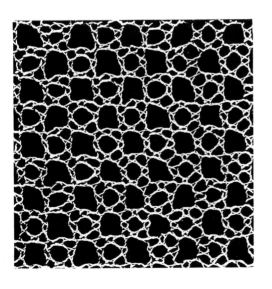

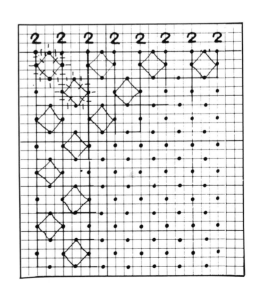

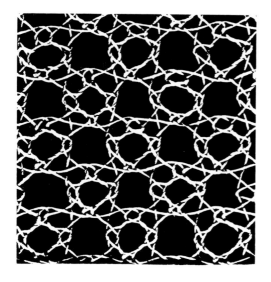

ROSE GROUND 6

3, 4, 5, 6 = 4 pin block

$$\begin{matrix} 1 & 3 & 2 \\ 4 & \diamondsuit & 5 \\ 7 & 6 & 8 \end{matrix}$$

1, 2, 7, 8 = intervening stitches

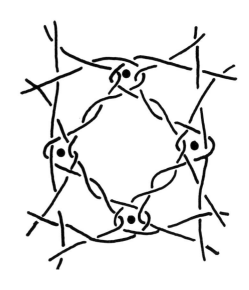

4 pin block: h.s., tw. 1, pin, h.s., tw. 1
intervening stitches: h.s. (no pin)
spaces and blocks alternated each row

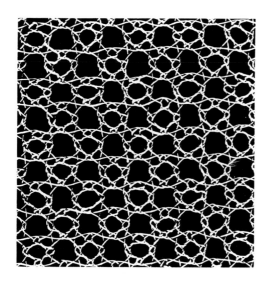

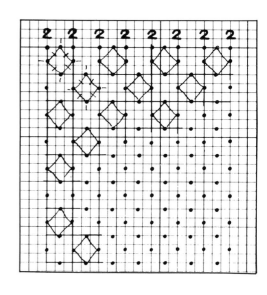

ROSE GROUND 7

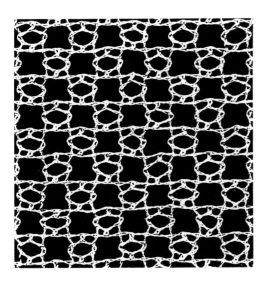

3, 4, 5, 6 = 4 pin block

```
    1 3 2
4  ◇  5
    7 6 8
```

1, 2, 7, 8 = intervening stitches

4 pin block: w.s., tw. 1, pin, w.s., tw. 1

intervening stitches: w.s., with tw. 1
    after it

spaces and blocks alternated each row

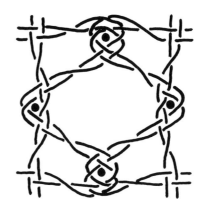

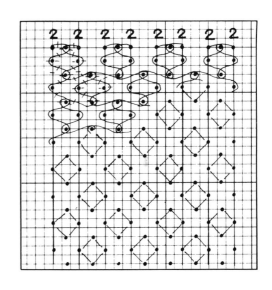

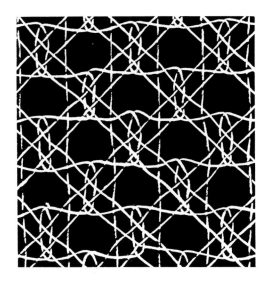

ROSE GROUND 8

3, 4, 5, 6 = 4 pin block

```
    1 3 2
4  ◇  5
    7 6 8
```

1, 2, 7, 8 = intervening stitches

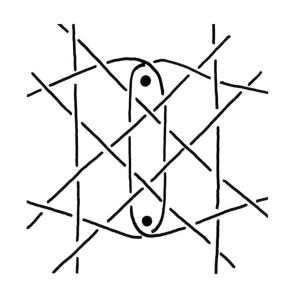

4 pin blocks:
  pinhole 3 — h.s., pin, h.s.
  pinholes 4 & 5 — h.s. (no pins)
  pinhole 6 — h.s., pin, h.s.

intervening stitches: h.s. (no pin)

spaces and blocks alternated each row

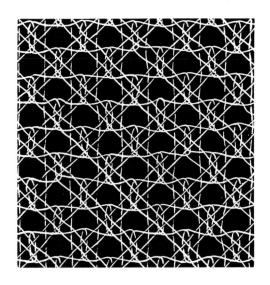

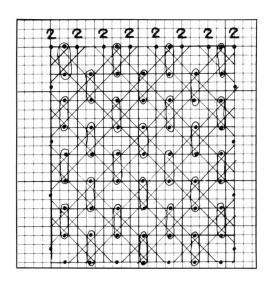

ROSE GROUND 9

3, 4, 5, 6 = 4 pin block

```
   1 3 2
4  ◇◇   5
   7 6 8
```

1, 2, 7, 8 = intervening stitches

4 pin block:
  pinhole 3 — h.s. (extra tw. 1 rt hd pr),
    pin, h.s.
  pinhole 4 — h.s. (extra tw. 1 to outside
    pr), pin, h.s.
  h.s. 2 middle prs
  pinhole 5 as 4
  pinhole 6 as 3

intervening stitches: h.s., pin, h.s.

spaces and blocks alternated each row

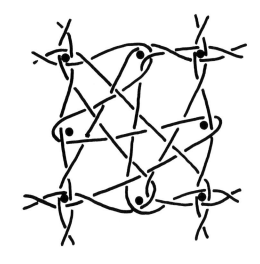

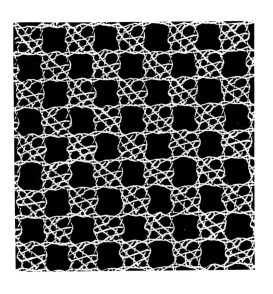

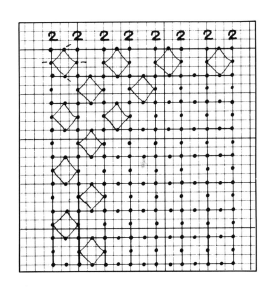

74

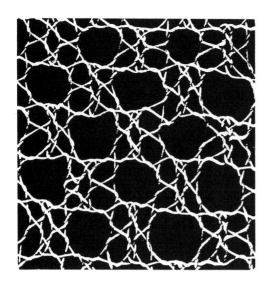

ROSE GROUND 10

3, 4, 5, 6 = 4 pin block

```
      1 3 2
  4  ◇  5
      7 6 8
```

1, 2, 7, 8 = intervening stitches

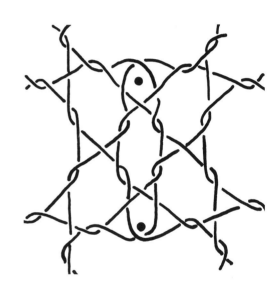

4 pin block:
   3 — h.s., pin, h.s., tw. 1
   4 and 5 — h.s., tw. 1
   6 — h.s., pin, h.s., tw. 1

intervening stitches: h.s., tw.1

spaces and blocks alternated each row

work horizontally only or work pulls

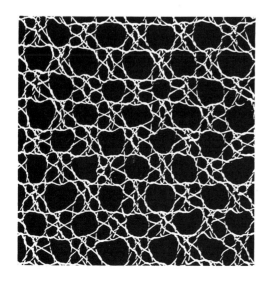

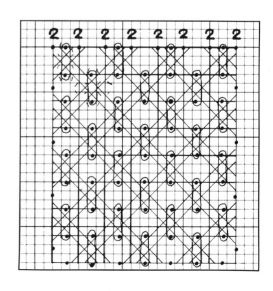

ROSE GROUND 11

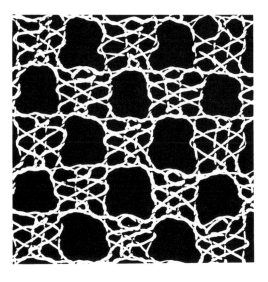

3, 4, 5, 6 = 4 pin block

```
   1 3 2
4  ◇  5
   7 6 8
```

1, 2, 7, 8 = intervening stitches

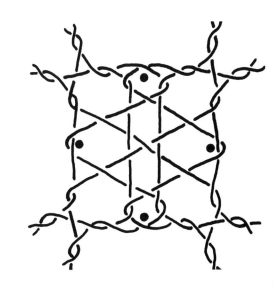

4 pin block:
    3 — h.s., tw. 1, pin, h.s.
    4 and 5 — h.s., tw. 1 outside pr, h.s.
      with 2 middle prs
    4 and 5 — close pins with h.s., tw. 1
      outside pr
    6 — h.s., tw. 1, pin, h.s., tw. 1

intervening stitches: h.s., tw. 1

spaces and blocks alternated each row

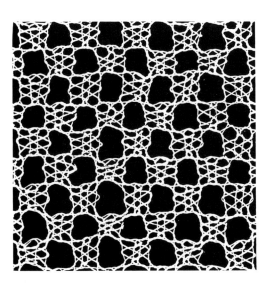

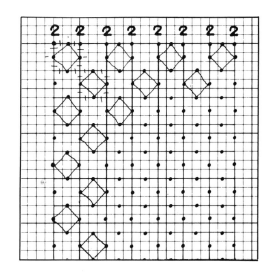

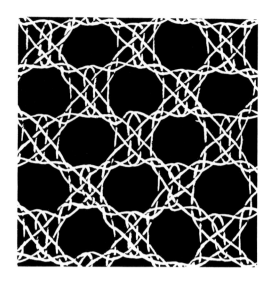

ROSE GROUND 12

3, 4, 5, 6 = 4 pin block

```
    1  3  2
4    ◇     5
    7  6  8
```

1, 2, 7, 8 = intervening stitches

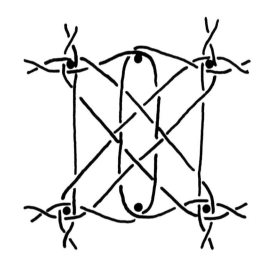

4 pin block:
    3 and 6 — h.s., pin, h.s.
    4 and 5 — h.s.

intervening stitches: h.s., pin, h.s.

spaces and blocks alternated each row

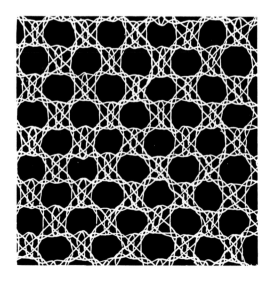

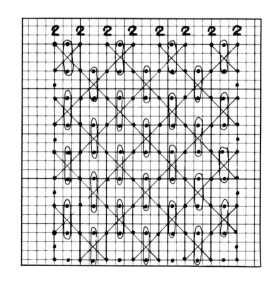

ROSE GROUND 13

3, 4, 5, 6 = 4 pin block

```
    1 3 2
4   ◇   5
    7 6 8
```

1, 2, 7, 8 = intervening stitches

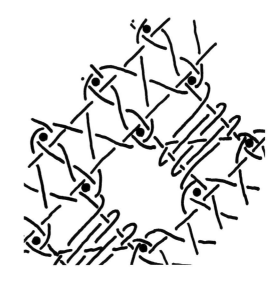

worked on diagonal only

4 pin block: h.s., pin, h.s. as usual *but* work h.s. 2 middle prs between pins numbered 4 and 5

h.s. 2 lt hd prs between blocks

prs between rows make tallies

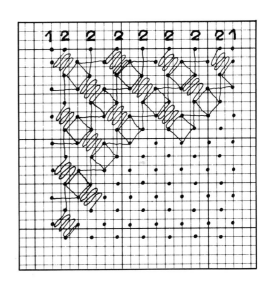

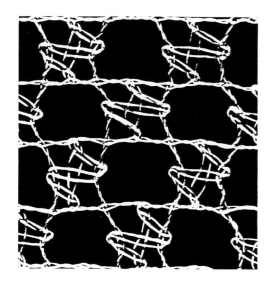

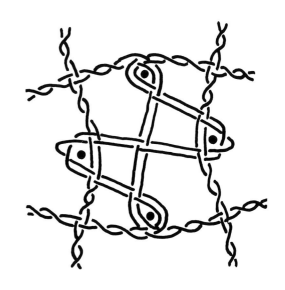

w.s. throughout

no twists in zigzag centres

tw. 2 all other horizontal and vertical
   lines

tw. 2 at winkie pins

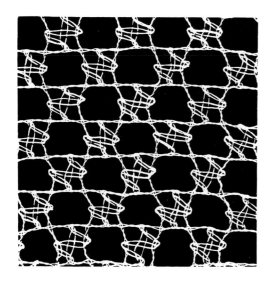

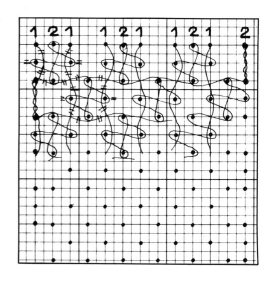

ROSE GROUND 15

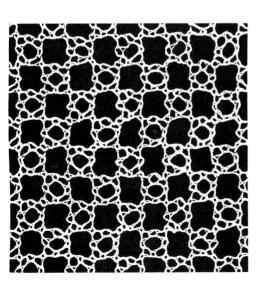

3, 4, 5, 6 = 4 pin block

```
    1 3 2
4    ◇    5
    7 6 8
```

1, 2, 7, 8 = intervening stitches

4 pin block and intervening stitches:
    h.s., tw. 1, pin, h.s., tw.1

spaces and blocks alternated each row

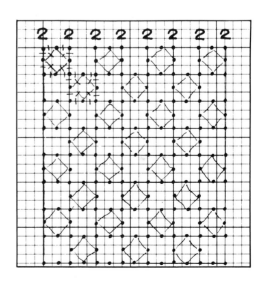

80

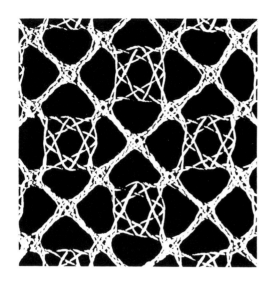

ROSE GROUND 16

3, 4, 5, 6 = 4 pin block

```
       1  3  2
    4   ◇    5
       7  6  8
```

1, 2, 7, 8 = intervening stitches

4 pin block: h.s., pin, h.s.

intervening stitches:
  pinholes 1 and 2 — w.s., tw. 1
  pinholes 7 and 8 — w.s.

braid x 4½ between joints

joints between braids:
  w.s. 2 middle prs
  w.s. 2 rt hd prs and 2 lt hd prs, pin,
    w.s. 2 middle prs

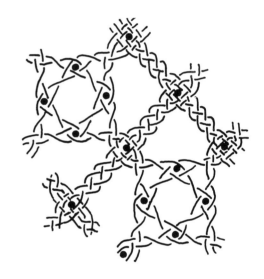

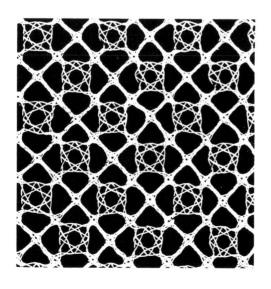

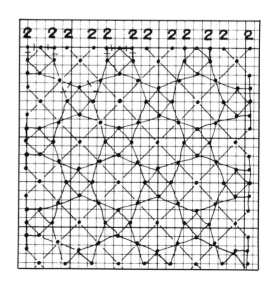

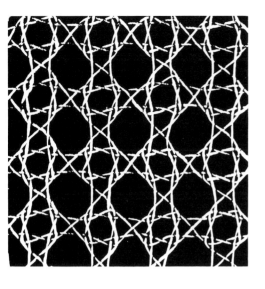

ROSE GROUND
WORKED STRAIGHT

3, 4, 5, 6 = 4 pin block

```
    1 3 2
4   ◇   5
    7 6 8
```

1, 2, 7, 8 = intervening stitches

use two horizontal workers at same time

h.s., pin, h.s., 1 & 2 & A & B

with both working prs work h.s. at X

h.s., pin, h.s., 3 & 4 & C & D continue to
  end

h.s. alternate squares Y & Z

work workers back as before: alternate
  squares and crosses

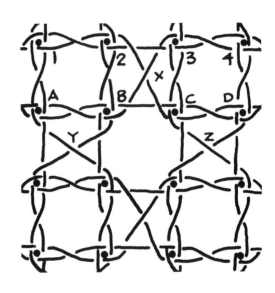

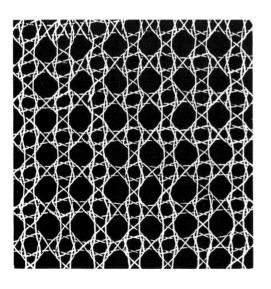

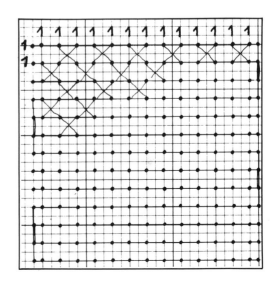

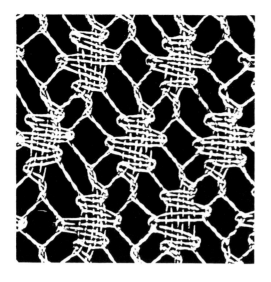

SIX LEGGED ZECCATELLO

This can also be done in half stitch.

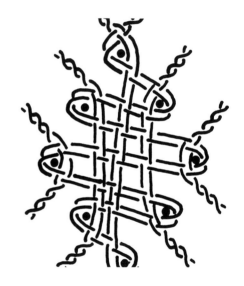

top rt hd leg — worker

w.s. back and forth picking up legs to
rt and lt until all 6 legs are in use,
then leave out legs lt and rt until
original 2 prs

tw. 1 workers at winkie pins

tw. 3 between diamonds

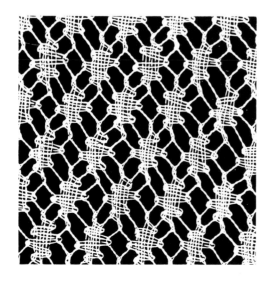

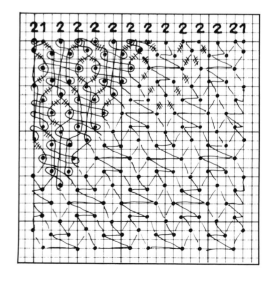

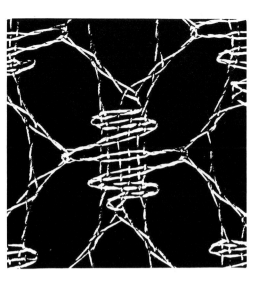

all verticals: tw. 2

all diagonals: tw. 1

joints at top and bottom of diamond: h.s., tw. 1, pin, cross

h.s., tw. 1, pin, h.s., tw. 1 between diamonds

w.s. through diamonds with tw. 2 round pin *except* at widest 2 points: tw. 3, w.s., pin, tw. 1, w.s., tw. 3

repeat at other side

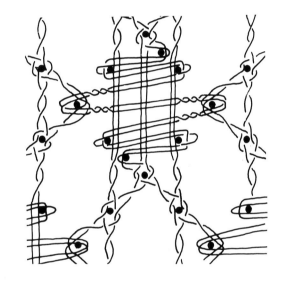

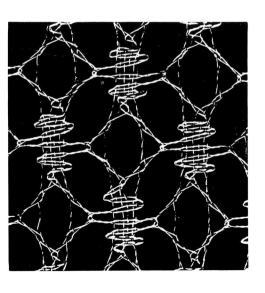

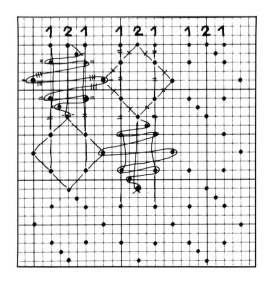

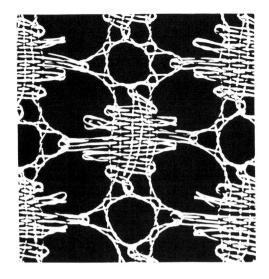

FOUR PIN MAYFLOWER

This stitch is also sometimes called Pig's Ear.

w.s. diamonds, tw. 2 workers at pinholes

tw. 2 passives and workers at bottom of diamonds

h.s., tw. 1, pin, h.s., tw. 1 at all other pinholes

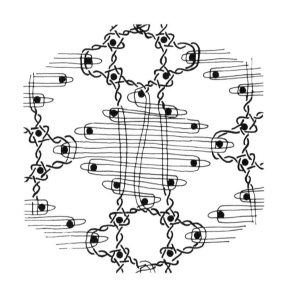

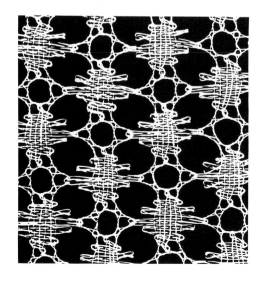

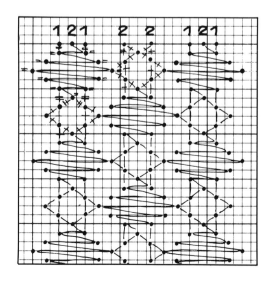

FOUR PIN MAYFLOWER WITH PINCHAIN

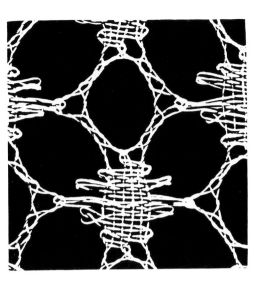

w.s. diamonds, tw. 2 workers at pinholes

tw. 2 passives and workers at bottom of diamonds

h.s., tw. 1, pin, h.s., tw. 1 at all other pinholes

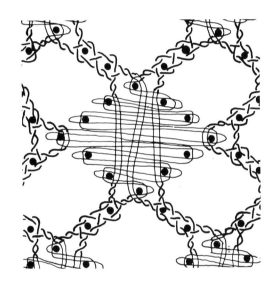

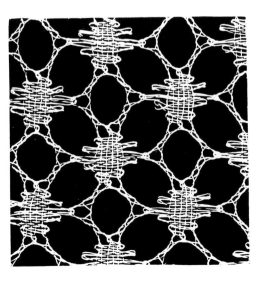

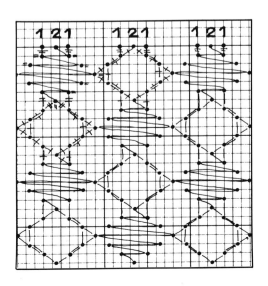

MAYFLOWER

w.s. diamonds, tw. 2 workers at pinholes

tw. 2 passives and workers at bottom of
  diamonds

h.s., tw. 1, pin, h.s., tw. 1 at all other
  pinholes

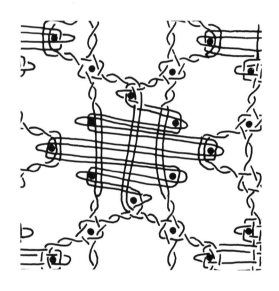

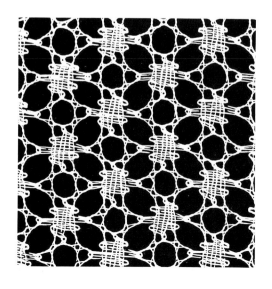

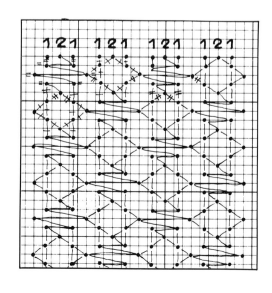

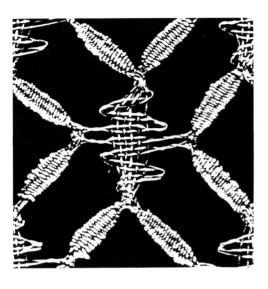

w.s. through diamonds with tw. 2 round
    pins except at widest 2 points: tw. 3,
    w.s., tw. 1, w.s., tw. 3

weave narrow leaves where indicated

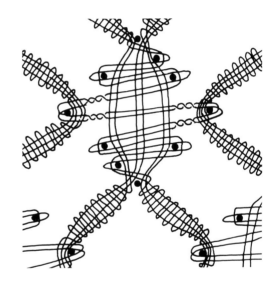

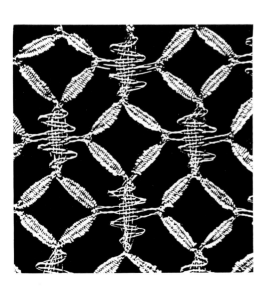

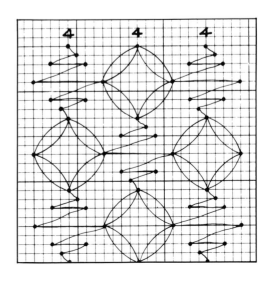

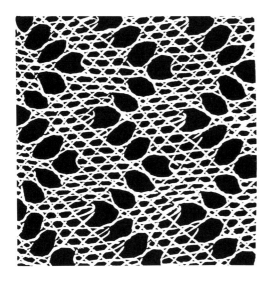

HALF STITCH ZIGZAG

this pattern is worked horizontally in sets

rt to lt zigzag set:
    (1) repeat the following x 3 —
        5 h.s. to lt, pin,
        4 h.s. to rt, pin,

    (2) tw. 1 3 legs on rt hd side
    (3) start next rt to lt zigzag
    (4) continue until end of horiz. set

lt to rt zigzag set:
    (1) repeat the following x 3 —
        3 h.s. to lt, pin
        4 h.s. to rt, pin

    (2) tw. 1 3 legs on lt hd side
    (3) start next lt to rt zigzag
    (4) continue until end of horiz. set

repeat these 2 sets until end

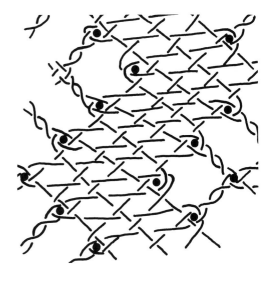

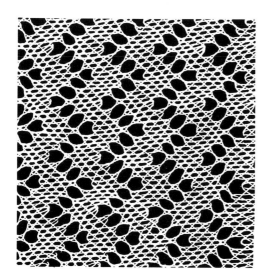

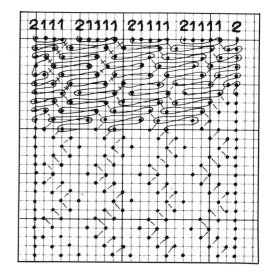

HALF STITCH DIAMONDS

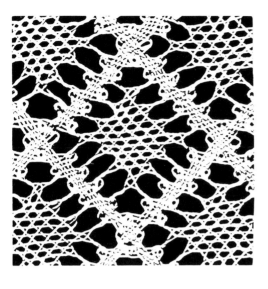

w.s. diagonal bars until 2 meet

w.s., pin, w.s.

w.s. these prs through their respective passives, tw. 1 both workers, pin and leave

w.s. all 4 passives through each other

w.s. workers back through respective passives again

w.s., pin, w.s. at bottom hole

continue w.s. back and forth, tw. 2 at each turn, adding legs one side and leaving out other side

tw. 2 all legs left out

h.s. diamond in middle

tw. 1 all legs after diamond

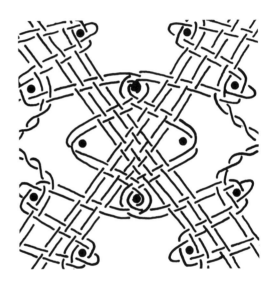

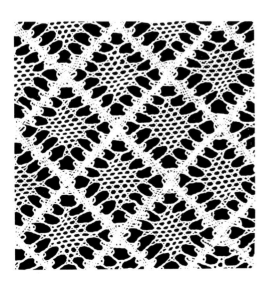

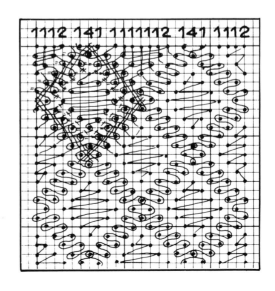

90

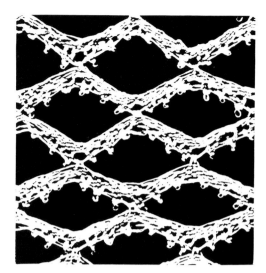

FESTOON

with 1 pr as workers, w.s. through 3
    passives, tw. 3, w.s. 1 passive, work
    picot

return through 1 passive, tw. 3, w.s. 2
    passives

work turning stitch: w.s. and h.s. with
    worker and last passive, then return

repeat 6 times

make sewing into centre of moon of
    previous row

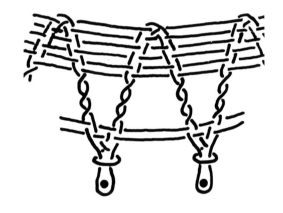

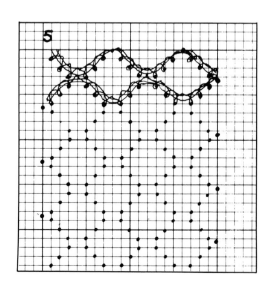

throughout motif, work back and forth
in w.s., at end of lines pin before last
w.s. where new worker is brought in
and old worker is left as passive

work as diagram — noting half lines only
near widest part

centre prs tw. 2: h.s., pin, h.s., tw. 1

half lines again, then work as diagram,
but leaving out prs at each pin

tw. 2 all legs before next motif

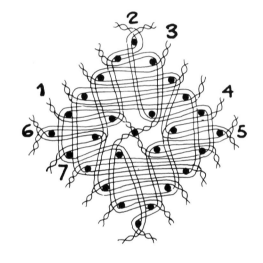

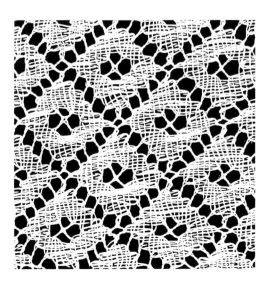

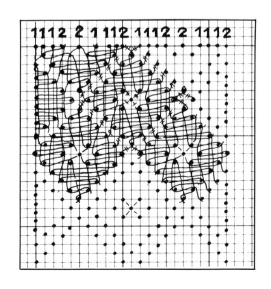

FLAGS

lt to rt diagonal braids:
   start with lt hd thread and weave it
   under and over next 7 threads — leave,
   repeat this move 8 times
   tw. 2 all 4 prs
rt to lt diagonal braids:
   start with rt hd thread and weave it
   over and under next 7 threads — leave,
   repeat this move 8 times
   tw. 2 all 4 prs

pin between prs

w.s., tw. 2 all 8 prs through each other

pin before starting new braids

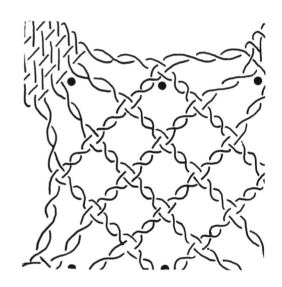

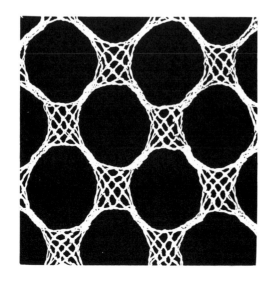

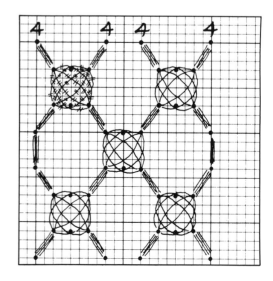

FINISH HALF STITCH DIAGONAL GROUND

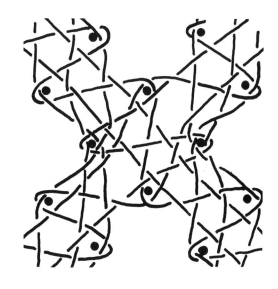

h.s. throughout with extra tw. at pinholes

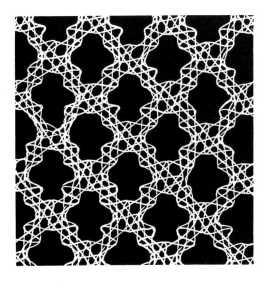

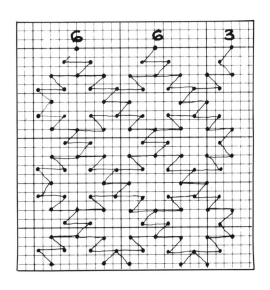

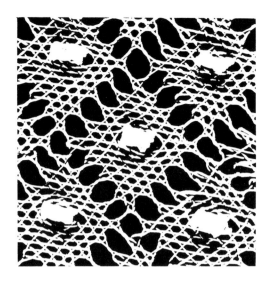

HALF STITCH DIAMOND WITH RAISED TALLIES

work diamonds in h.s. picking up prs
   each side until first widest point reached

untwist 2 centre prs and make a raised
   tally

put 2 support pins below tally

finish h.s. diamond leaving out prs after
   2nd widest point has been completed

tw. 1 between diamonds

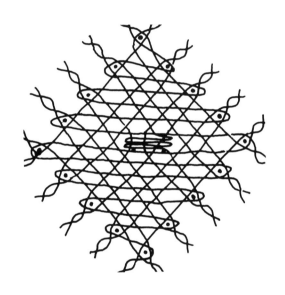

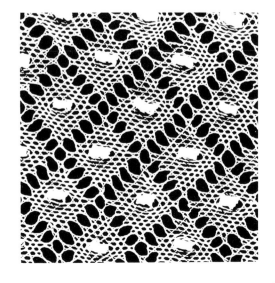

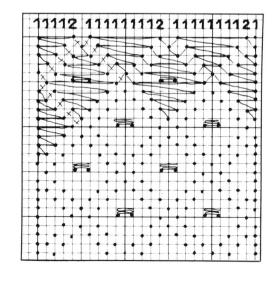

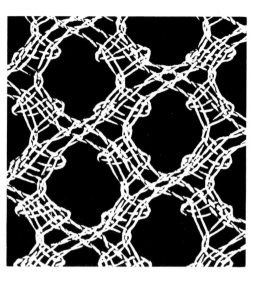

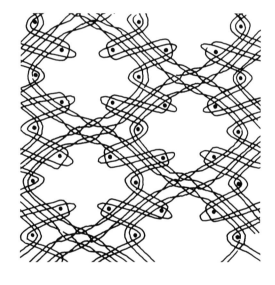

w.s., pin, w.s. each side of circle

w.s., tw. 2, w.s. at winkie pins

tw. 1, w.s., tw. 1 at grill squares top and
    bottom of circles

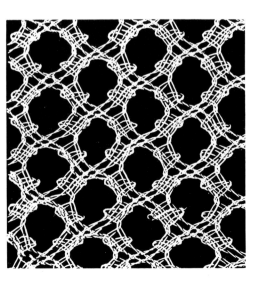

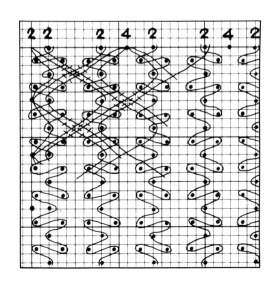

DANISH WHOLESTITCH DIAGONAL GROUND

w.s. and tw. 1 throughout

tw. 2 at winkie pins

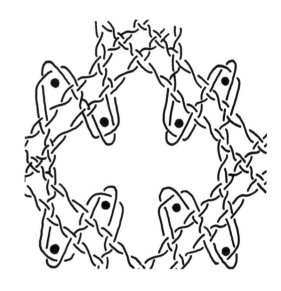

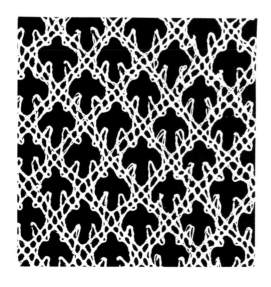

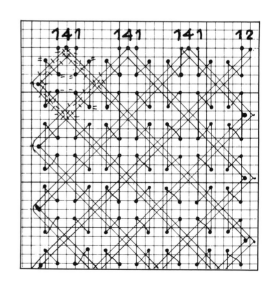

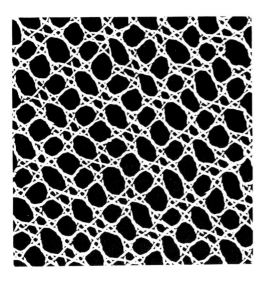

SMALL HALF STITCH DIAMOND GROUND

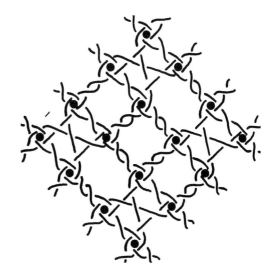

h.s., pin, h.s. top pin of little diamonds

h.s. rt hd pr with new pr from rt, pin

h.s. to lt picking up new pr from lt, pin

h.s. back through 2 prs, pin

h.s., tw. 1

tw. 1 other 2 legs

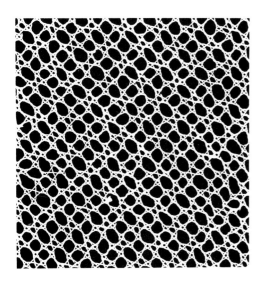

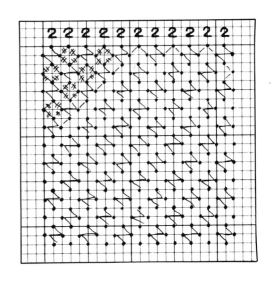

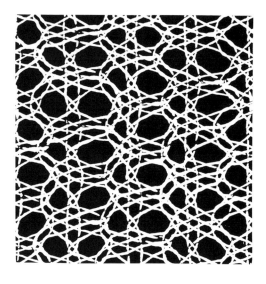

TWELVE THREAD ARMURE

h.s., pin, h.s. 2 middle prs

*h.s. centre lt through 2 lt hd prs

h.s. centre rt through 2 rt hd prs

pin between 2 outside prs each side

h.s. 2 middle prs

repeat from * again, but without pins

h.s. centre lt through 1 lt hd pr

h.s. centre rt through 1 rt hd pr

h.s., pin, h.s. 2 middle prs

tw. 1 2 legs each side

note: in a Mechlin sample — top and
    bottom pinholes — h.s., tw. 2, h.s.
    and legs tw. 2

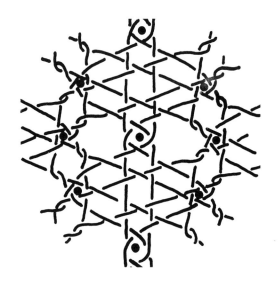

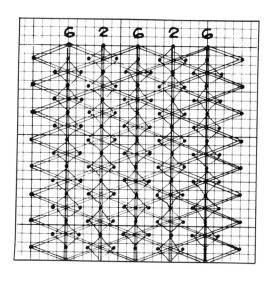

EIGHT THREAD ARMURE – BINCHE

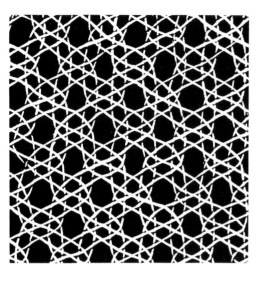

made in 4 pin groups throughout

h.s., pin centre 2 prs

h.s., pin 2 lt hd prs and 2 rt hd prs

h.s. centre 2 prs

h.s. 2 lt hd prs and 2 rt hd prs

h.s., pin centre 2 prs

diagram shows 4 groups

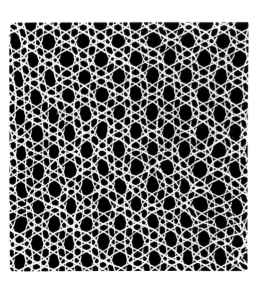

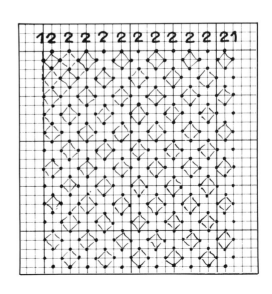

1 2 2 2 2 2 2 2 2 2 1

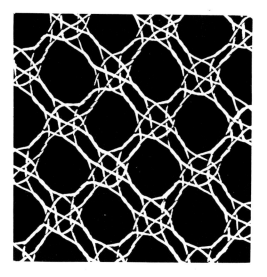

EIGHT THREAD
ARMURE – MECHLIN

h.s., pin 2 centre prs and 2 rt hd prs

h.s. 2 lt hd prs

h.s., pin 2 centre prs

h.s. 2 rt hd prs and 2 centre prs

h.s., pin 2 lt hd prs

tw. 2 all 4 legs

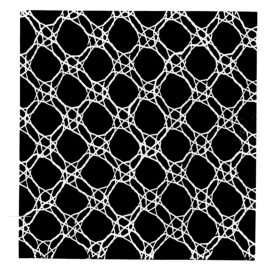

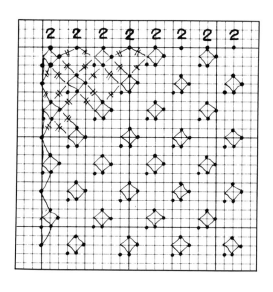

CORD GROUND

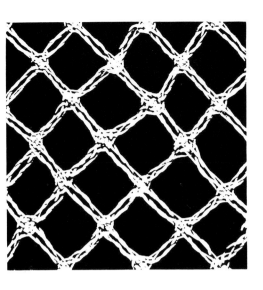

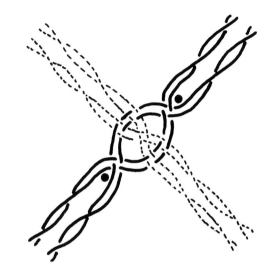

tw. 2 all legs between crossings

pin between solid diagonal prs

w.s. these 2 prs

w.s. top solid pr through both dotted prs

w.s. 2 dotted prs

w.s. bottom solid pr through 2 dotted prs

w.s. 2 solid prs

pin, tw. 2

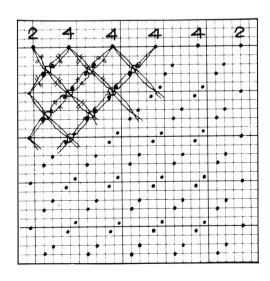

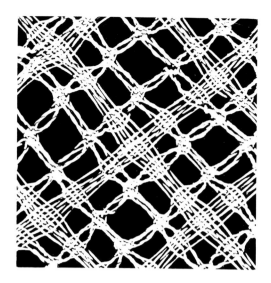

CORD GROUND IN UNTWISTED FRAME

diagonal frames:
> w.s. through each other and all spider legs

cord ground centres:
> tw. 2, *pin, w.s. at top of spider on diagonals from right to left
>
> diagonals from left to right — tw. 2 before and after spider
>
> w.s. both prs through first pr from spider
>
> w.s. through each other, then through other pr from spider
>
> w.s. spider prs, pin, tw. 2*

repeat from * to * once again

make another group as above before completing frame

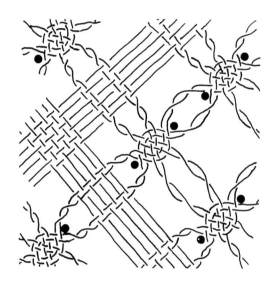

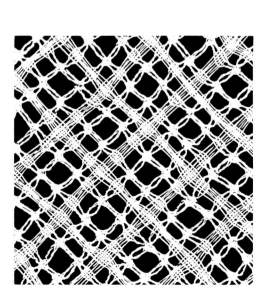

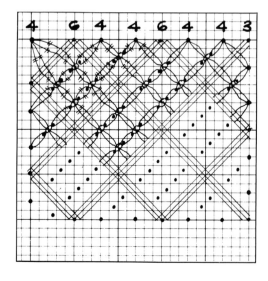

HALF STITCH CLOVER GROUND

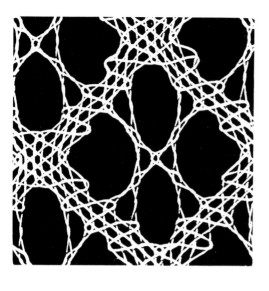

junction of diagonals:
    h.s., pin, h.s. at top pin
    h.s. centre lt to lt hd side, pin, h.s. 2
        outside prs
    h.s. centre rt to rt hd side, pin, h.s. 2
        outside prs
    h.s. 6 central prs through each other

pin, h.s. 2 central prs

central motif:
    tw. 1 prs left out of diagonals
    h.s., tw. 1, pin, h.s., tw. 1 at each
        pinhole

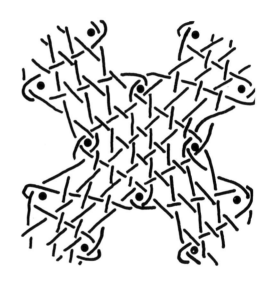

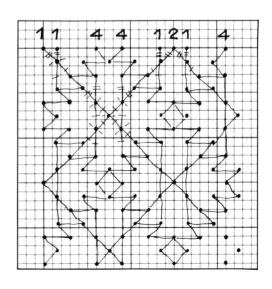

THORNS

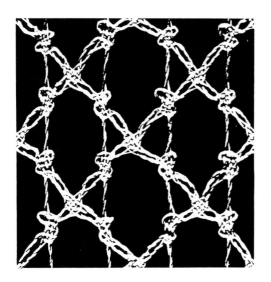

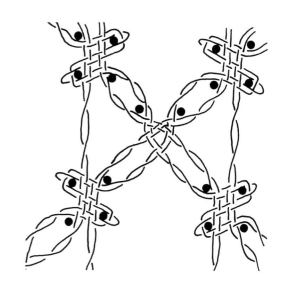

w.s. throughout

tw. 2 at winkie pins

tw. 2 all verticals and diagonals between
blocks

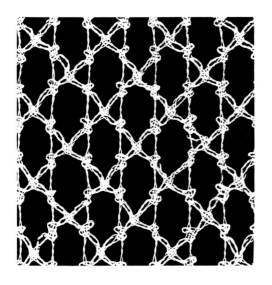

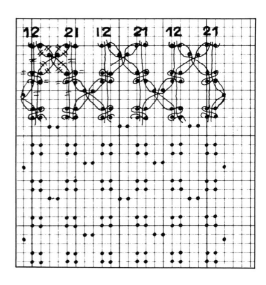

HONEYCOMB BARS AND PINCHAIN

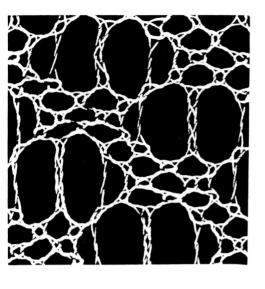

honeycomb stitch throughout:
    h.s., tw. 1, pin, h.s., tw. 1

work diagonal bars first, then pinchain
    (3 consecutive honeycomb stitches)
    and crosses as shown

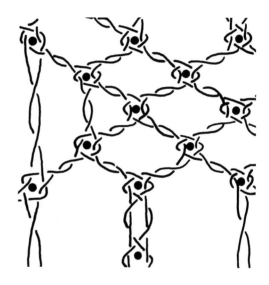

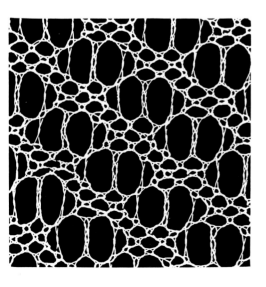

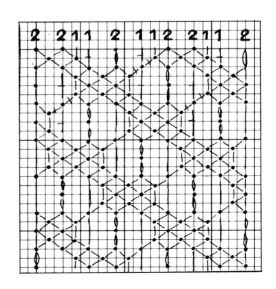

HALF STITCH HONEYCOMB

h.s., tw. 1, pin, h.s., tw. 1 between h.s. blocks

h.s., pin, h.s. top of h.s. block, h.s. back and forth, tw. 1, pin at sides, ending — h.s., pin, h.s.

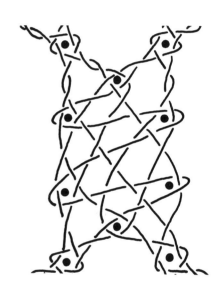

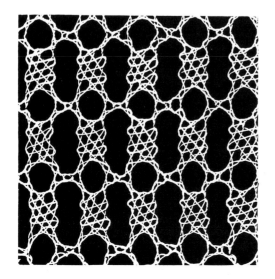

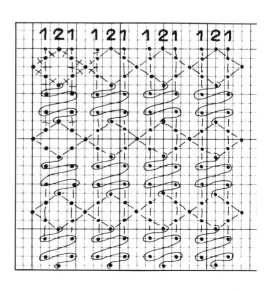

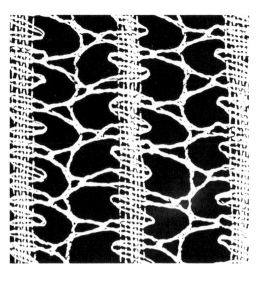

w.s. workers back and forth through vertical bars, tw. 2 at winkie pins, until junction with zigzag centre

h.s. x 3 centre prs, tw. 1 both

*h.s. x 3 rt hd pr with worker from rt hd bar, tw. 1 both

h.s. x 3 vertical pr with lt hd pr from last stitch, tw. 1 both

h.s. x 3 lt hd pr with workers from lt hd bar, tw. 1 both

h.s. x 3 rt hd pr with vertical pr, tw. 1 both

repeat from * for zigzag centre

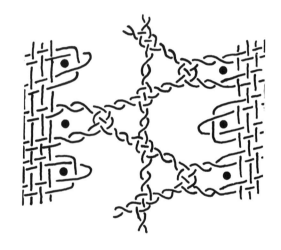

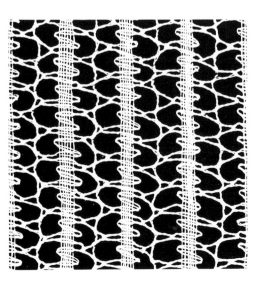

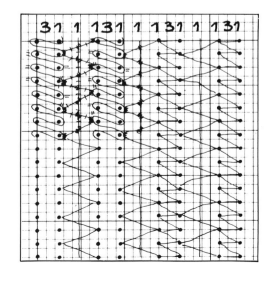

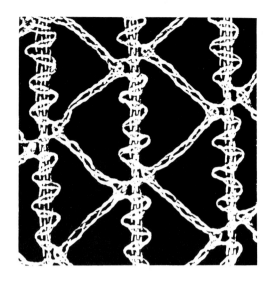

WHOLESTITCH BARS WITH PINCHAIN

w.s. workers back and forth through
   passive, tw. 2 at winkie pins

pinchain: h.s., tw. 1, pin, h.s., tw. 1, pin,
   h.s., tw. 1, pin, h.s., tw. 1 and leave

junction of pinchain with bars:
   tw. 2 worker from bar
   w.s. worker through pinchain prs
   pin between pinchain prs
   w.s. pinchain prs
   tw. 2 all prs
   w.s. pr nearest bar through 2 passive
   prs — this then becomes new worker

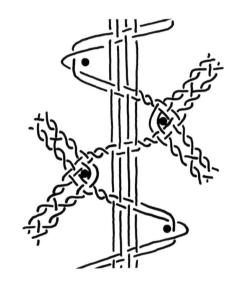

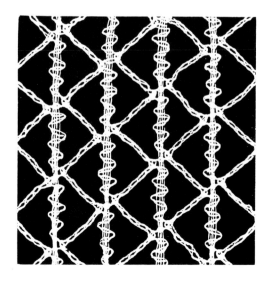

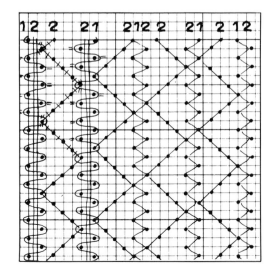

VALENCIENNES 1

The typical diamond look can be achieved by using this technique but with a wider pricking.

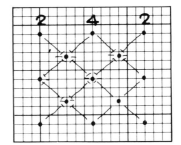

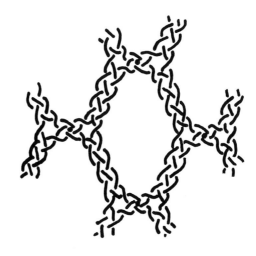

braid 4 times

h.s., pin, h.s. centre prs

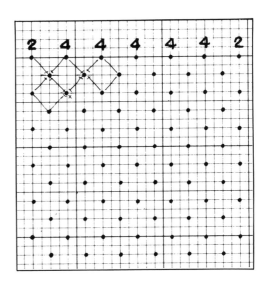

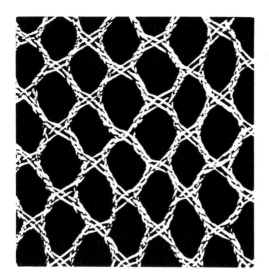

VALENCIENNES 2

braid 3½ times

no twists in the centre prs, work w.s.
   with pin in middle

tw. 1 hanging prs

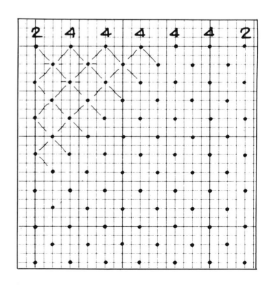

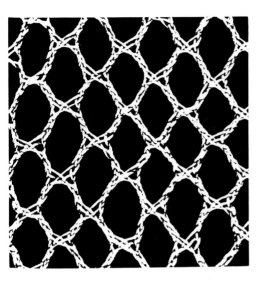

braid 3½ times

w.s. with pin in middle centre prs

tw. 1 centre prs and hanging prs

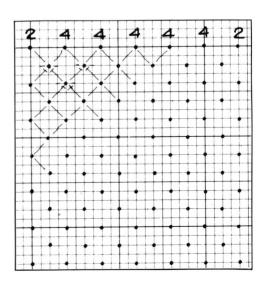

VALENCIENNES 4

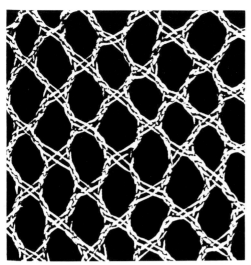

braid 3½ times

no twists throughout join

w.s. with pin in middle

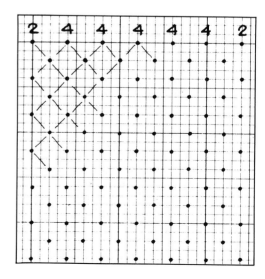

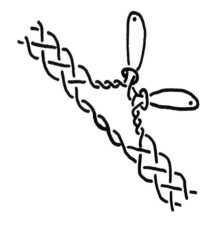

braid x 5, tw. 3, 2 large knotted picots
with pins to hold shape, braid x 5

lazy join between braids

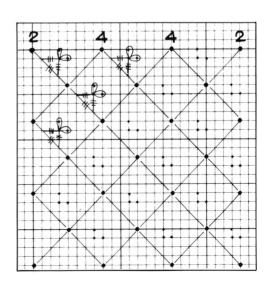

VALENCIENNES WITH PICOTS 2

joint of braids
    tw. 1 inner prs, w.s. with pin in middle,
    tw. 1 centre prs, tw. 1 outside prs

taking one inner and one outer pr braid
    x 3½, double picot, braid x 3½, double
    picot, braid x 3½

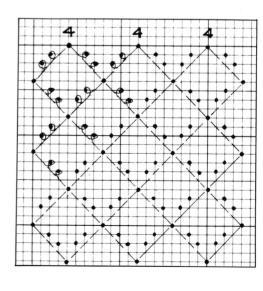

braid to lowest point of diamond

take rt hd pr of lt hd braid, tw. 3, make picot, pin each end of picot, tw. 1 both prs

make lazy join with other two prs

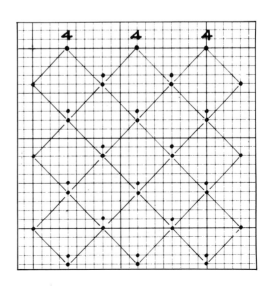

VALENCIENNES WITH PICOTS 4

braid x 5½, double large knotted picots
   with h.s. between

braid x 5½

lazy join between braids

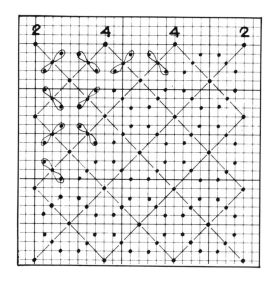

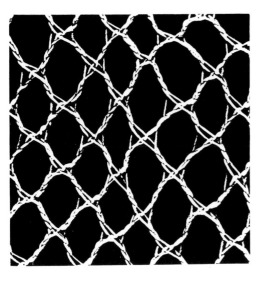

THREE THREAD
VALENCIENNES

plait x 3

w.s. 4 threads nearest centre pin

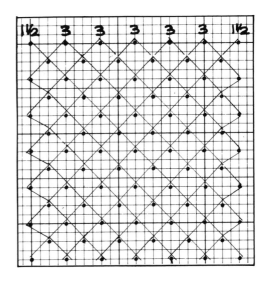

ROUND VALENCIENNES

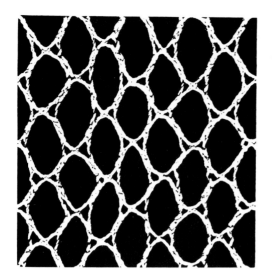

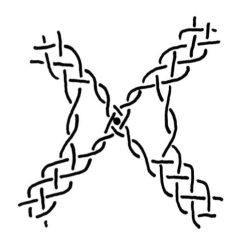

braid 3½ times

tw. 2 all prs

w.s. with pin in middle, tw. 2 inner prs

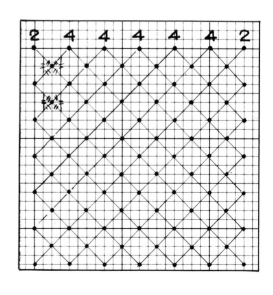

TRESSES WITH OPEN HOOKED JOINTS

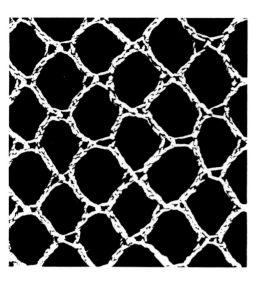

braid x 4, tw. 2 each pr

rt hd pr place pin between threads, braid x 3½, tw. 2 each pr

lt hd pr place pin between threads, braid x 3½

joint is made where next braid zigzags to meet it

tw. 1 lt hd pr — make sewing into former hole with this pr, tw. 1, idle pr tw. 2

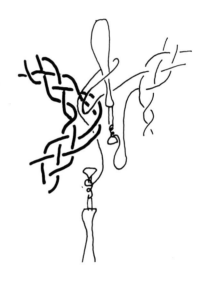

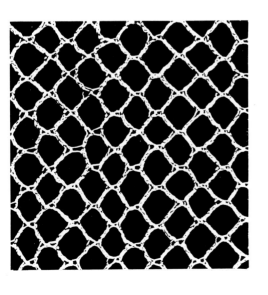

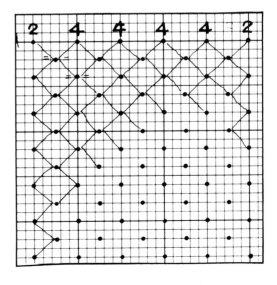

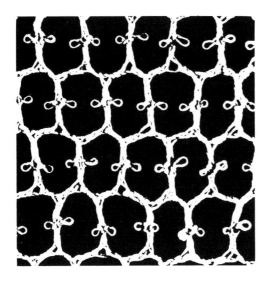

HEXAGONAL BRAID WITH PICOTS 1

can only be worked diagonally, right to left

prs have to be added at rt hd side as well as at top, then tied out on lt hd side and bottom

* work down long vertical side — braid x 3½, make knotted picot each side, braid x 3½, pin between prs

braid x 3½ along the rt to lt short side

make sewing with top pr of braid into lt hd pinhole of previous row, gently pull to make sewing same length as braid x 3½

sew round this new bar again

continue until end of row

then start again at top of new row

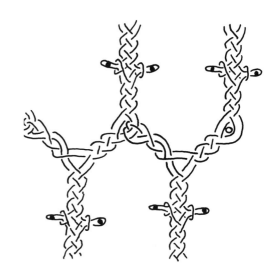

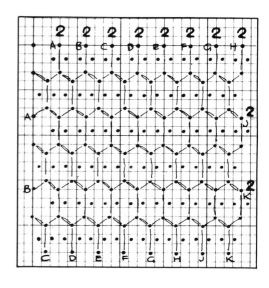

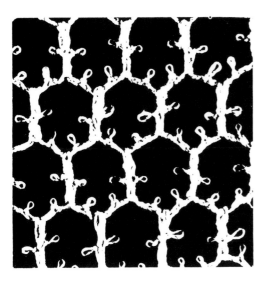

HEXAGONAL BRAID
WITH PICOTS 2

braid x 3½ between knotted picots
  throughout

start at A, braid to pinhole B, pin braid
  around it up to C, make sewing, braid
  up beyond C (this keeps sewing tight),
  then fold this braid down so that it
  rests on top of braid B-C, after picot
  on rt make sewing under lower braid
  to secure both braids together, continue
  braid to B, make another sewing at B
  and braid around pin at D — continue

not an easy pattern to keep tidy with its
  3 sewings for each vertical bride

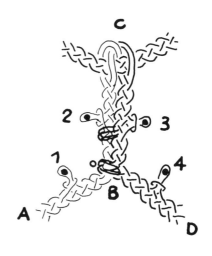

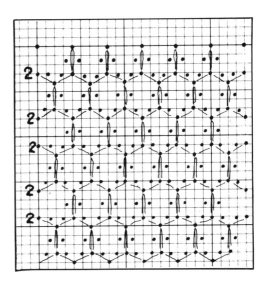

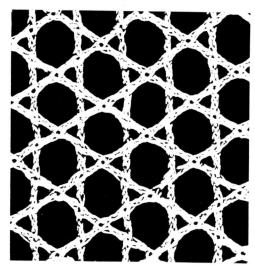

BRAIDED KAT STITCH

braid x 3 and lazy join throughout

made with pin in middle on diamond
grid and without pins elsewhere

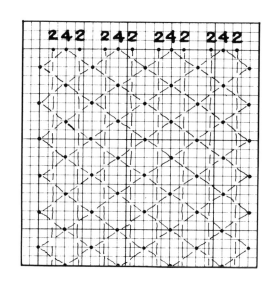

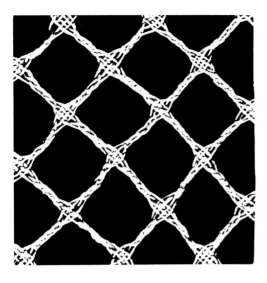

Braid and cross can be made with three twists before and after the wholestitch for a fuller effect.

braid x 5½

pin between prs

w.s. 2 centre prs

w.s. 2 lt hd prs

w.s. 2 rt hd prs

w.s. 2 centre prs

pin between prs before commencing
    new braiding

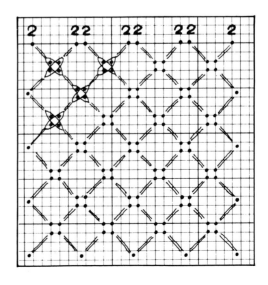

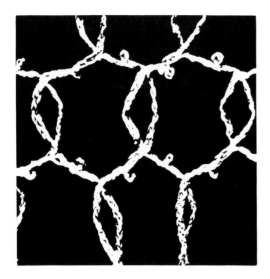

BRAIDED LEAVES 1

braid throughout

where 2 braids meet at top and bottom
pins of leaf, cross 3 threads of 1 braid
over 3 threads of other braid, cross
single threads left *under* the above 2
sets of 3 threads

pin out each side of leaf to give shape

picot on rt of both braids before starting
next row

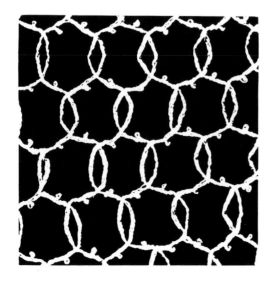

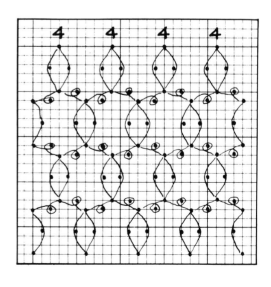

BRAIDED LEAVES 2

This pattern can also be made on this pricking to give a diamond effect.

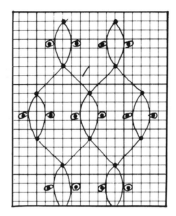

braid with knotted picots

lazy join at all junctions, with pin in
middle

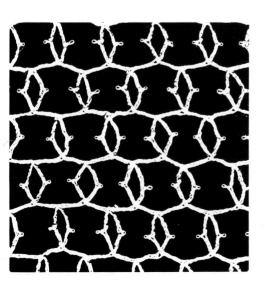

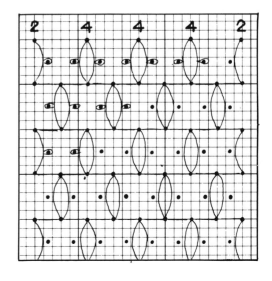

BRAIDED SQUARES

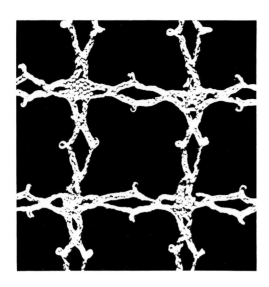

braid until double picots

work double picots

braid until pinhole, pin

work lazy join with all 4 prs from braids

braid x 2½

w.s. through cross braids

braid x 2½

pin

lazy join, repeat from the beginning

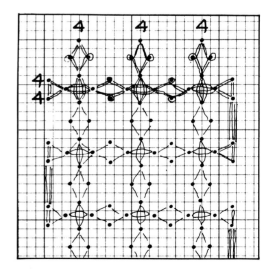

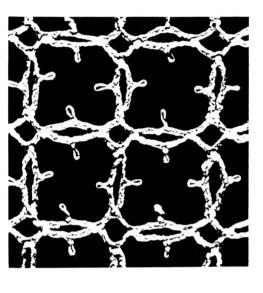

BRAIDED LEAVES
WITH PICOTS

work with only one braid throughout

braid with knotted picots

tw. 2 at pinholes and continue to plait
   (this makes hole for sewing)

double sewings throughout

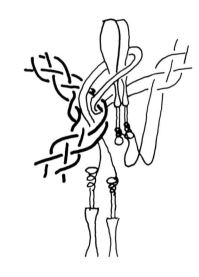

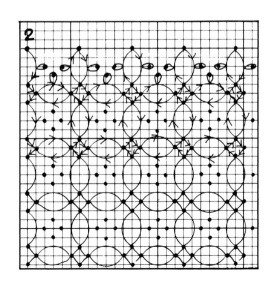

HEXAGONAL BRAIDED LEAVES

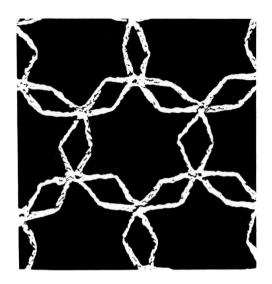

work horizontal leaves by using 2 sets
of braids, one for the rt hd and one for
the lt hd edge of leaf

make lazy join with pin in middle, at base
of leaf, continue to end of line, take
both braids down to next horizontal
line, and work back to base of vert.
leaf, using only one braid, braid up
one side of leaf and do double sewing
into the join of pr of leaves above it

braid down second side of leaf, make
another lazy join, with pin, at base as
close as possible to first lazy join of
horizontal leaf

continue

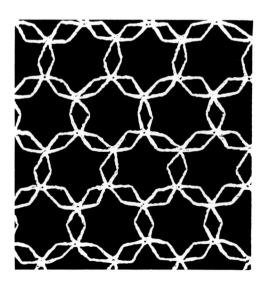

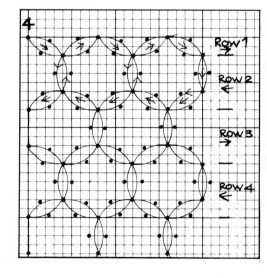

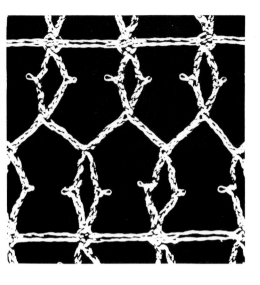

braid leaf shapes with knotted picots

lazy join together braids at bottom of
  leaf

using each pr (from braids) as single
  threads, w.s. both horizontals

lazy join verticals before starting braids
  again

tw. 4 horizontals between joints

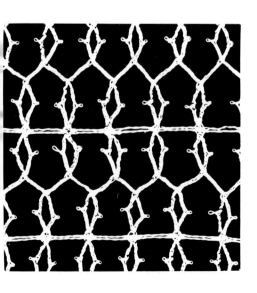

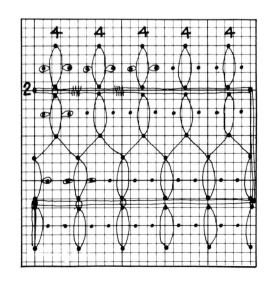

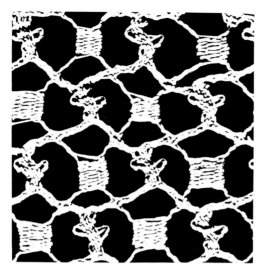

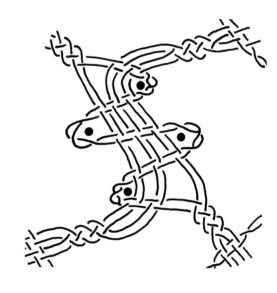

braid x 4 before and after flowers

flowers: rt hd pr of lt hd braid becomes
the worker, w.s. through 3 prs back
and forth, tw. 3 at winkie pin and
ending bottom rt ready to start next
braid

tw. 3 before each tally

tallies: weave back and forth ending
on rt hd side, tw. 3 both prs, w.s. pr
with weaver first to secure the tally

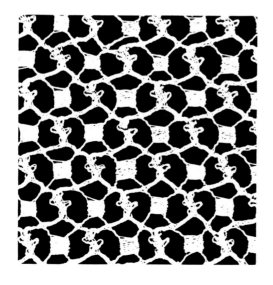

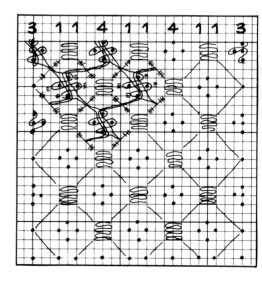

MOULINET

each leg is braided with knotted picots
    each side and half way down each braid

each braid is opened out (with pin) and
    w.s. through other opened braids

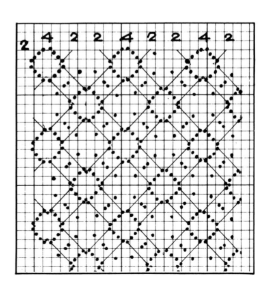

DEVONSHIRE FOUR PEARL FILLING

This filling is also sometimes called Blossom or Rose.

rt hd pr of lt hd braid, picot on right, w.s.

2 middle prs: w.s., tw. 1

2 rt hd prs: w.s., picot to the right, w.s.

2 lt hd prs: w.s., picot to the left, w.s.

2 middle prs: tw. 1, w.s.

2 rt hd prs: w.s., picot to the left

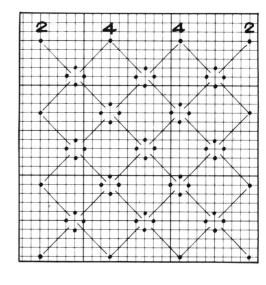

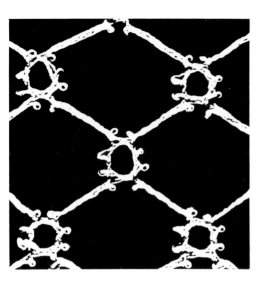

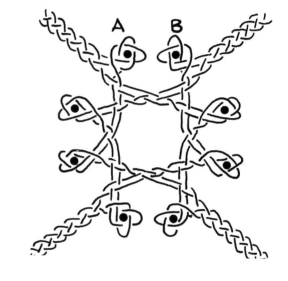

DOUBLE APPLE BLOSSOM

133

braid to pin A

work lt hd picot at A, tw. 1, w.s., repeat
   on rt hd side at B, but reversed

w.s. centre prs, tw. 1

2 lt hd prs w.s., double picot on lt, tw. 1
   w.s.
double picot again on lt, w.s., tw.1 rt hd
   pr only
repeat on rt hd side but reversed
w.s. centre prs
w.s. 2 lt hd prs double picot on rt of
   this join, tw. 1

braid

repeat on rt hd side but reversed

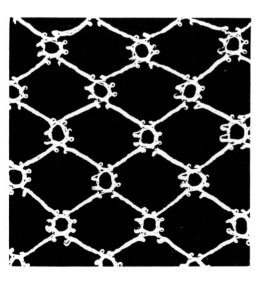

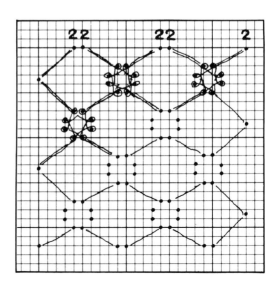

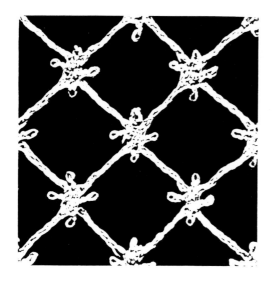

WHOLESTITCH APPLE BLOSSOM

braid legs

pin between prs

lt hd pr of lt hd braid w.s., picot at top
  pin, w.s. to right, leave
w.s. 2nd from rt to lt and picot on lt
  hd side
w.s. back to right and picot on right
w.s. to left, leave
pin and take lt hd vertical w.s. to right,
  picot at bottom
w.s. to far right, pin between prs

tw. 1 all 4 prs before braiding

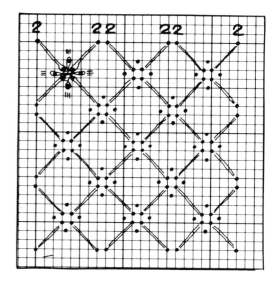

FLOWER CENTRED BRAID

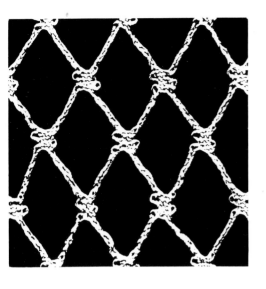

braid two legs

with rt hd pr of rt leg (pin between prs.) w.s. through its own pr and lt hd prs

tw. 1, pin, w.s. back through to rt, tw. 1, pin, w.s. back, put pin between last 2 prs

tw. 1 each pr, braid each leg again

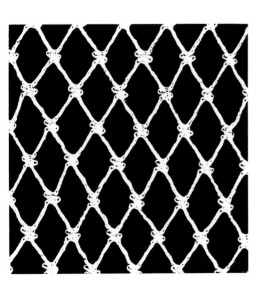

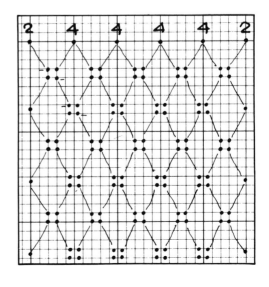

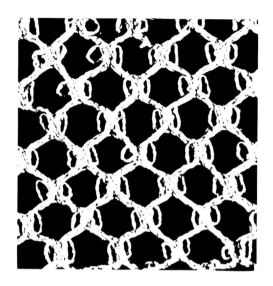

BRAID AND WINKIE PINS

braid until w.s. brick

lt hd pr of rt hd braid becomes worker

w.s. through 2 prs to lt pin, tw. 6, pin

w.s. to rt, pin, tw. 6, pin

w.s. through 2 prs to lt, then braid with
   next pr until next w.s. brick

braid 2 rt hd prs to next w.s. brick

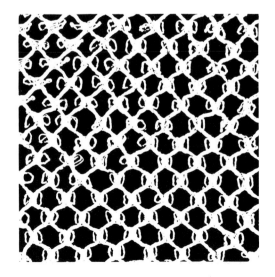

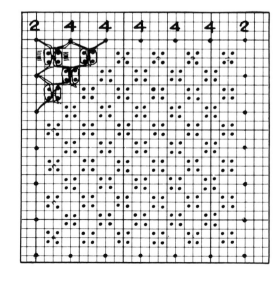

BRAID WITH RAISED KNOTS

braid both legs

h.s., pin, h.s. centre 2 prs

braid x 9 centre prs, place on one side, leave

w.s. outside prs under braid, place on outside again

with small stick, raise up braid and remove pin from start and place through last crossing of braid, replace pin in same hole

with 1 centre pr and its outside pr braid next leg, repeat on other side

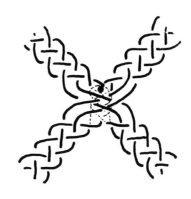

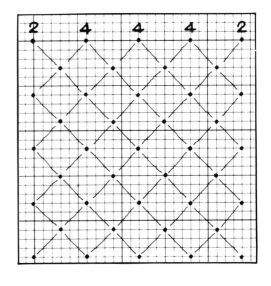

138

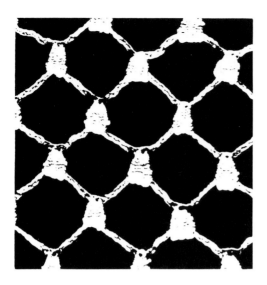

BRAID WITH RAISED LEAVES

braid both legs

h.s., pin, h.s. centre 2 legs

make long leaf, place on one side

w.s. outside prs under leaf, place on outside again

with small stick, raise up leaf and remove pin from start and place between leaf prs, replace in same hole

with 1 centre pr and the adjacent outside pr, braid next leg, repeat on other side

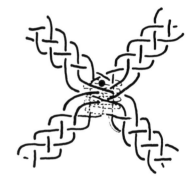

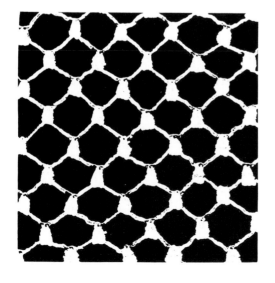

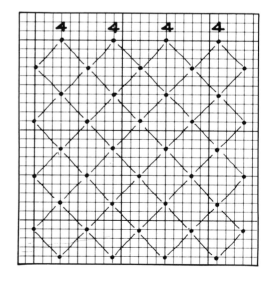

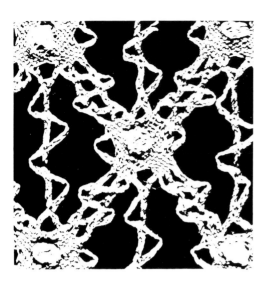

BRAID AND RAISED TALLIES

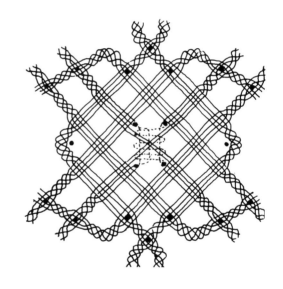

all braids crossed by lazy joins, put pin
   in middle until next joint is made

w.s. in middle of spider

isolate centre 4 prs

centre 2 for tally and next 2 prs cross with
   w.s. behind tally and take up same
   position after tally

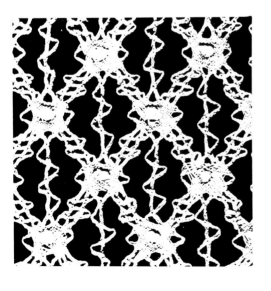

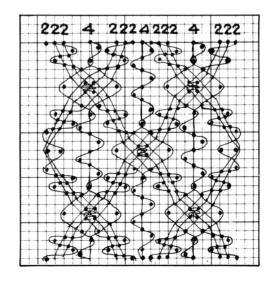

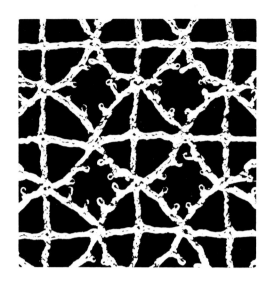

BRAIDED DIAMONDS AND SQUARES

braid with knotted picots

lt hd diagonal braid w.s. through vertical
braid then w.s. through rt hd diagonal
braid, pin, w.s. rt hd braid back through
vertical braid

where diagonals meet horizontals, w.s.
2 diagonal braids then w.s. horizontals
through

lazy join with pin in middle at other
junctions

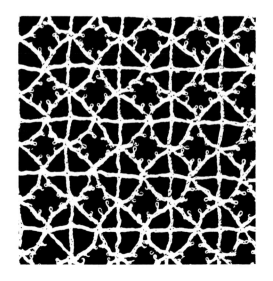

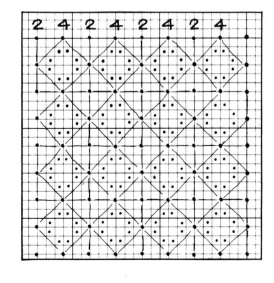

CATHERINE WHEEL

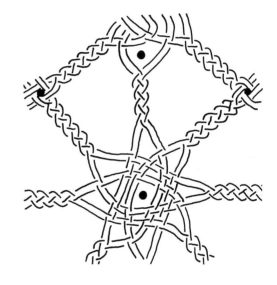

(2) Devonshire pearl filling:

  rt hd pr of lt hd braid, picot on right,
    w.s.
  2 middle prs — w.s., tw.1
  2 rt hd prs — w.s., picot to the right,
    w.s.
  2 lt hd prs — w.s., picot to the left,
    w.s.
  2 middle prs — tw. 1, w.s.
  2 rt hd prs — w.s., picot to the left

vertical 6 pr leg:
  divide into 3 groups of 2 prs each and use
  as 3 single threads, plait, at side pinhole
  picot with pr taken from the outside
  edge of plait, continue to top of wheel
top of wheel:
  lay plait flat and taking inner 2 prs,
  w.s. a pr outwards on each side through
  the outer 2 prs
braid throughout, lazy join with pin in
  middle at outer edge of wheel
wheel centre:
  using prs as single threads, cross inner
  prs of horiz. and lt hd diag. pr, cross inner
  prs of vert. and rt hd pr, w.s. prs through
  each other, cross inner prs as before
Devonshire pearl filling (see above rt)
  where diagonals meet
braid and picot horizontal between wheel

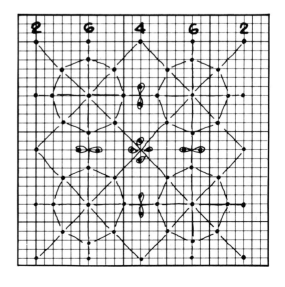

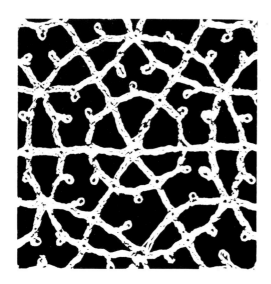

WHEEL WITH LEAVES

(2) six thread cross:
 use each pr as single threads — cross
 centre 2 threads, pass top horizontal
 thread over and under twice, twist both
 diagonal prs, pin between prs, then
 bottom horizontal thread under and
 over twice, twist middle 2 threads

(1) braid and double picot throughout
 double sewings at lt & rt of wheel and at
  top of vertical leaf
 six thread cross at centre of wheel (see
  above)
 lazy join with pin in middle at all other
  junctions; tw. 2 lower pr when there
  is to be a sewing later
 horizontal braid works through leaves,
  then top half of wheel, through
  diagonals, work back through centre
  to beginning of circle, sew and complete
  bottom half of circle, sew and braid to
  next wheel
 with 2 sets of braids work both top and
  bottom line of horizontal leaves, lazy
  join after each leaf, after 2nd horizontal
  leaf, top pr works up lt hd side of vertical
  leaf, sew into join of leaves above,
  return down rt hd side, lazy join as
  close to last lazy join as possible

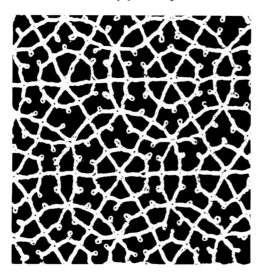

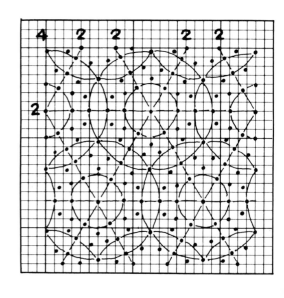

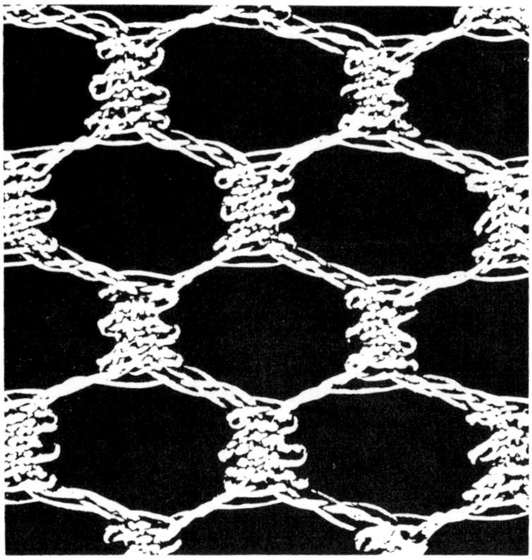

DEVONSHIRE WALL FILLING

when worker has been worked from rt to lt the last time at end of brick, the worker pr is passed under passive pr and w.s. again

then that pr works across to next brick

w.s. between bricks elsewhere

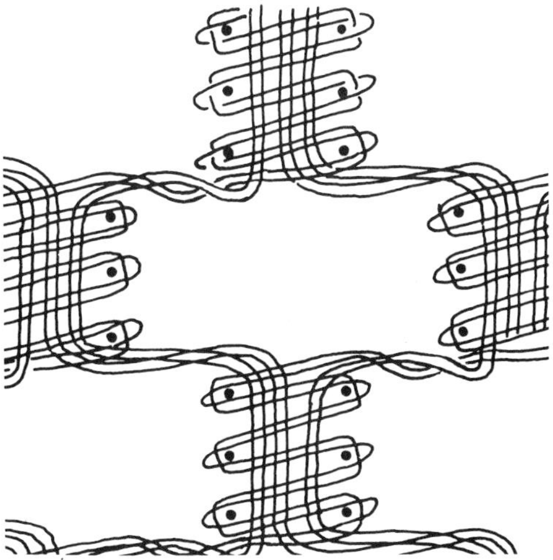

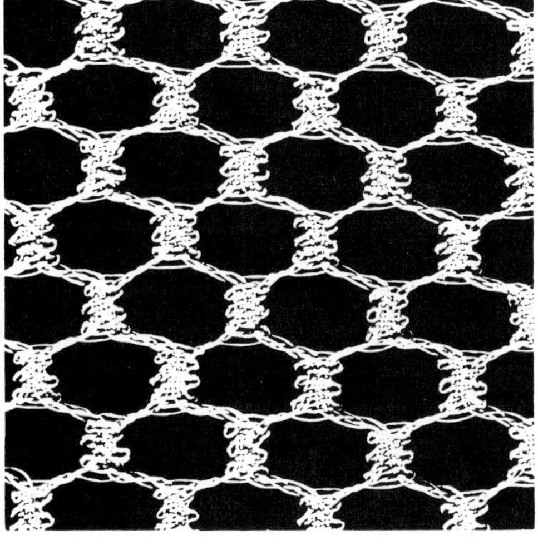

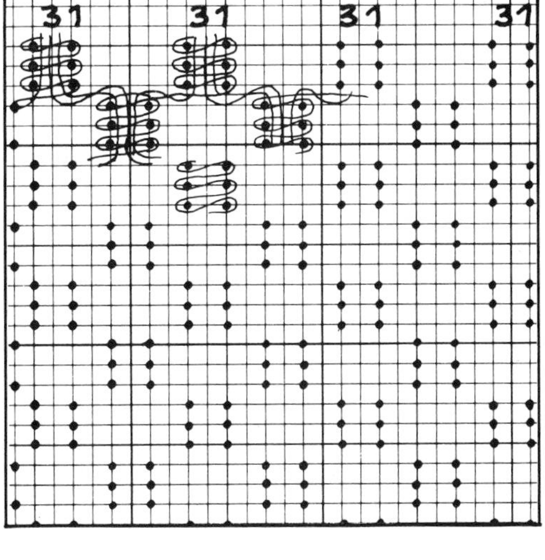

BRICK AND PICOTS

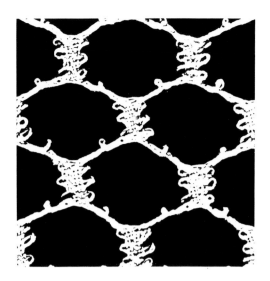

braid with double picot until brick

tw. 2 at winkie pins

weaver taken from rt hd pr of rt hd braid,
  weaves back and forth ending on the
  lt hd side

braid with lt hd pr of lt hd braid

braid 2 rt hd prs

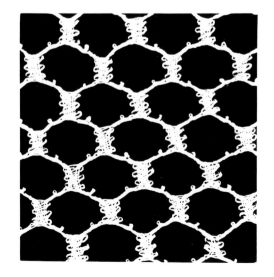

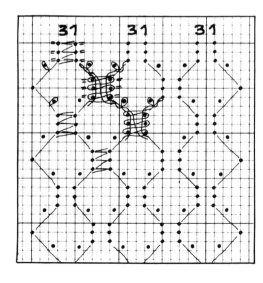

THREE BRAID CROSSING

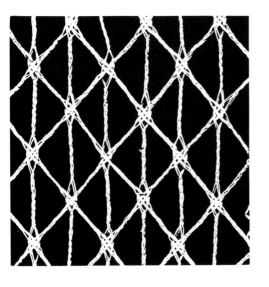

braid until 3 braid crossing ending with prs untwisted

pin between prs

work each pr as single thread, make sure these do not get twisted during the crossing

take centre lt pr under, then over 2 lt hd prs

take centre rt pr over, then under 2 rt hd prs

cross 2 centre prs

repeat these three moves again

take centre lt pr under next pr to left

take centre rt pr over next pr to right

pin between prs before starting braids

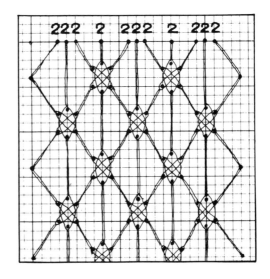

FOUR BRAID CROSSING

braid until 4 braid crossing, ending with prs untwisted

pin between prs

work each pr as single thread, make sure these do not get twisted during the crossing

*h.s. centre prs
h.s. lt hd prs
h.s. rt hd prs*

repeat from * to * twice more

h.s. centre prs once more

uncross all prs before braiding

pin between prs, braid until next crossing

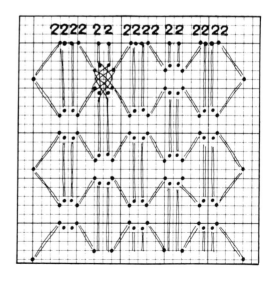

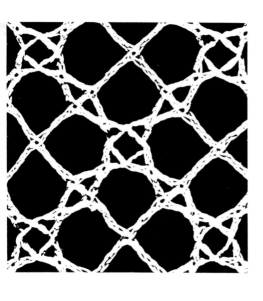

BRAIDED FLOWER MOTIF

braid throughout

lazy join at all junctions except centre
  diamonds of flower motif

at top and bottom pin of diamond cross
  3 threads of one braid over 3 threads
  of other braid, cross single threads
  left *under* the above 2 sets of 3 threads

at lt and rt side of diamond twist 3 threads
  of one braid over 3 threads of other
  braid, twist single threads left *under*
  the above 2 sets of 3 threads

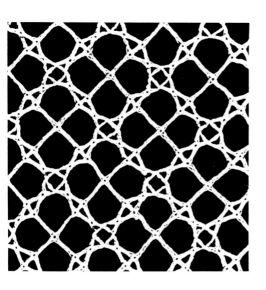

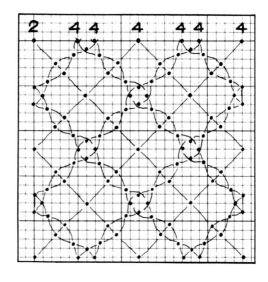

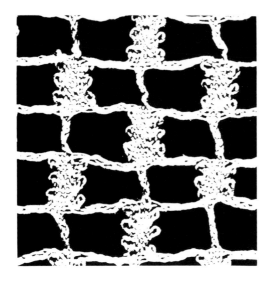

BRICK AND BRAID

braid until brick

bottom pr of rt hd braid becomes worker

weave back and forth, tw. 2 at winkie
pins and ends at bottom lt hd side

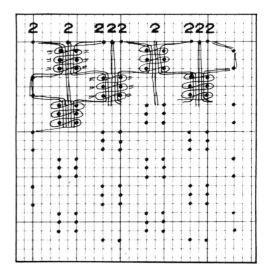

TWISTED BRICK WITH BRAID

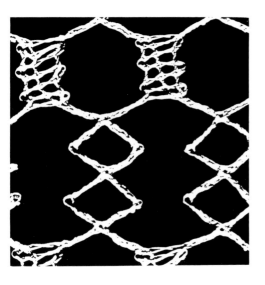

braid diamonds

lazy join where 2 braids cross

corner points: tw. 3 outside pr, pin, tw. 1
   inside pr, continue braiding until bricks

tw. 1, w.s. throughout bricks

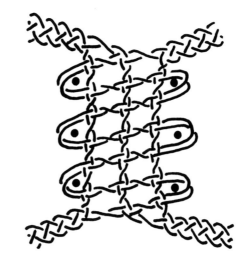

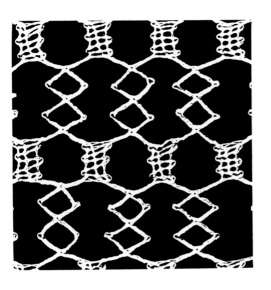

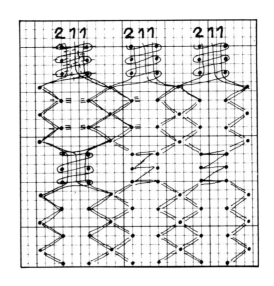

150

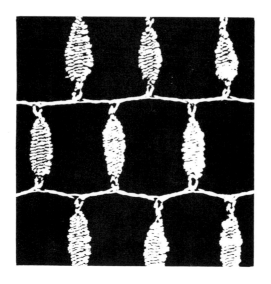

DEVONSHIRE PIN FILLING 1

This filling can also be made with square ended tallies, using the same method as below excluding the wholestitch at the top and bottom of the leaf.

top of leaf:
    w.s., pin, tw. 3, w.s., tw. 1

weave leaf as usual

bottom of leaf:
    w.s., pin, tw. 3, w.s., tw. 3

1 pr from each leaf above makes next
    leaf below

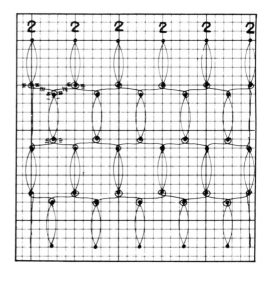

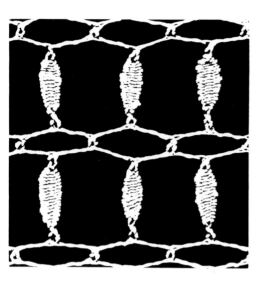

DEVONSHIRE PIN FILLING 2

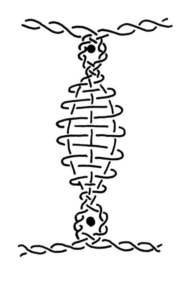

at pinholes between leaves:
    w.s., tw. 3, pin, w.s., tw. 3

top of leaf: w.s., pin, tw. 3, w.s., tw. 1

weave leaf as usual

bottom of leaf: w.s., pin, tw. 3, w.s.

divide prs at bottom of each leaf, tw. 3

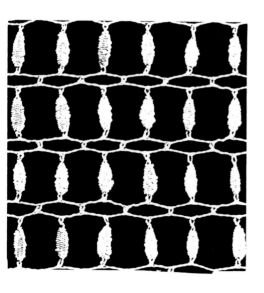

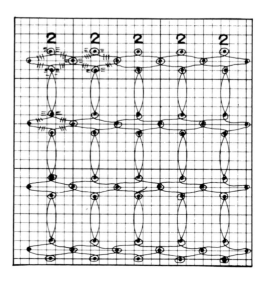

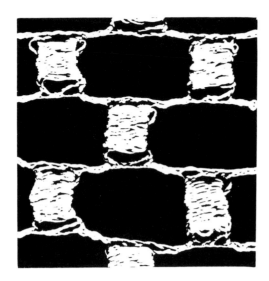

RAISED WALL TALLIES

braid both legs, tw. 2 all 4 prs

w.s., tw. 2 two centre prs

w.s. two lt hd prs, pin between, tw. 2 outside pr

repeat on rt hd side

w.s., tw. 2 outside prs through each other, pin

make raised tally

w.s. outside prs back through tally prs, tw. 2, then w.s. through each other again

tw. 2 all 4 prs before commencing braid

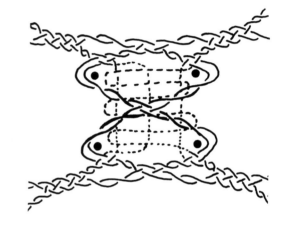

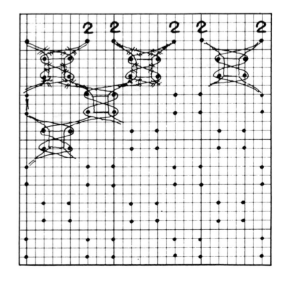

braid until brick

w.s. lt hd pr of rt hd braid to lt through the single pr and 2 lt hd prs, tw. 2, pin

w.s. back through all 4 prs, tw. 2 and pin

lift up 2 centre prs (for tally)

w.s., tw. 2, w.s., tw. 2, pin — twice

make raised tally

w.s. worker through all 4 prs, tw. 2, pin — twice, ending on rt hd side

braid to next brick

work single vertical pr with twists and knotted picots

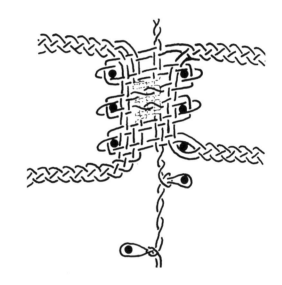

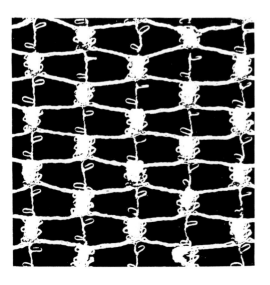

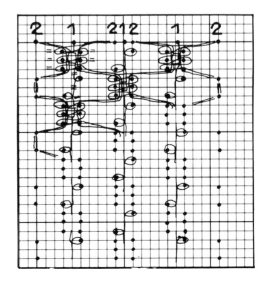

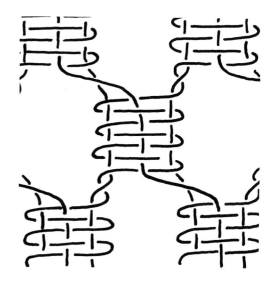

NO PIN FILLING

using the thread on far rt as weaver, weave back and forth ending on lt hd side

this way the weaver becomes the weaver for the next tally below left, which helps to keep its shape

tw. 2 weaver with its adjacent thread

tw. 1 bottom rt hd pr

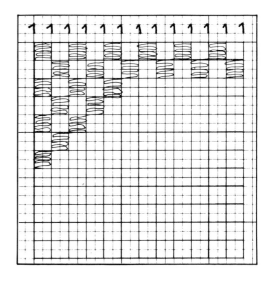

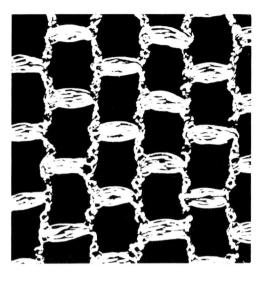

DEVONSHIRE CUSHION FILLING

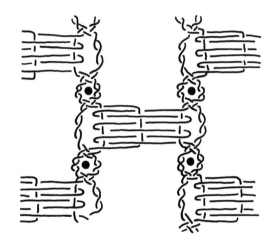

w.s., tw. 3, pin, w.s. at all pinholes between
   tallies

tw. 1 before and after tallies

work tally

tw. 3 outside prs hanging each side of
   tally

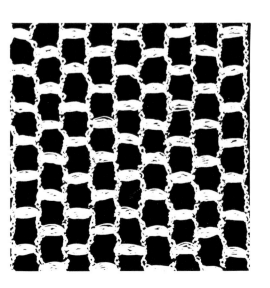

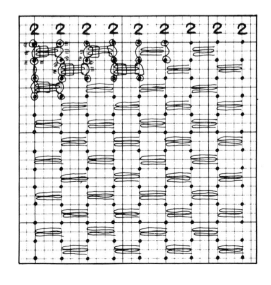

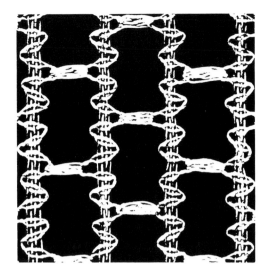

WHOLESTITCH CUCUMBER

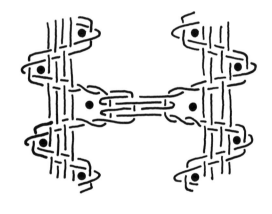

w.s. back and forth through vertical
  passives

tw. 2 at winkie pins

tw. 2 before and after tallies except bottom
  pr with weaving thread — tw. 3

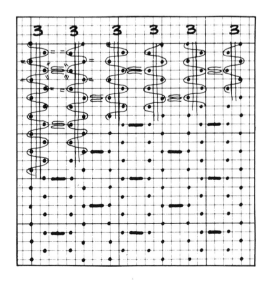

HALF STITCH CUCUMBER

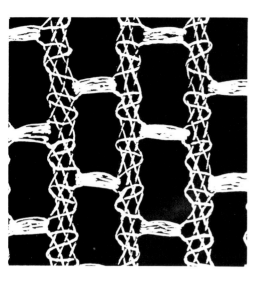

h.s. back and forth through passives

tw. 1 at winkie pin

tw. 2 before and after tallies

the shape of the tally is more easily
   retained if the weaver thread starts and
   finishes on the same side

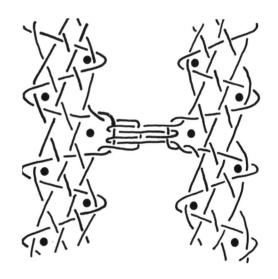

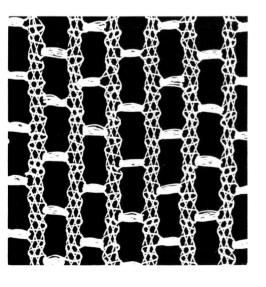

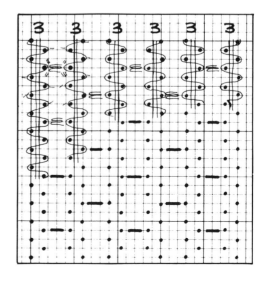

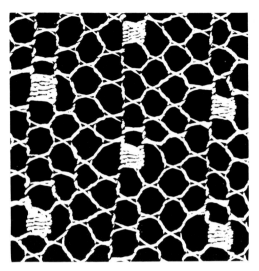

POINT D'ESPRIT

h.s., tw. 2, pin between the pairs

work tallies with two pairs

tw. 3 both prs at end of tallies and
    continue ground

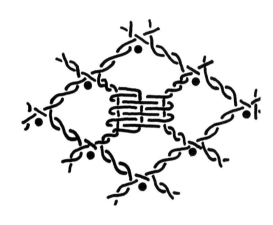

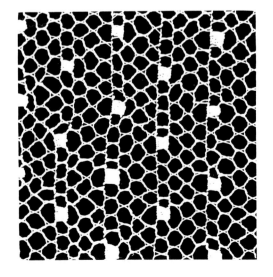

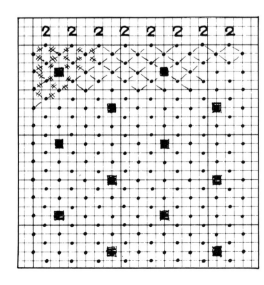

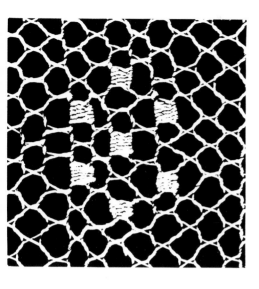

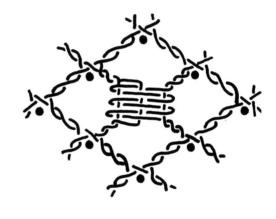

DECORATIVE POINT D'ESPRIT

h.s., tw. 2, pin between the prs

work tallies with 2 prs

tw. 3 both prs at end of tallies and
    continue ground

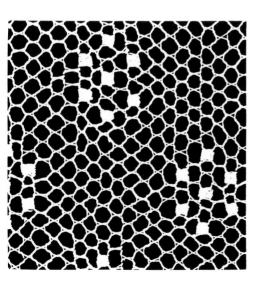

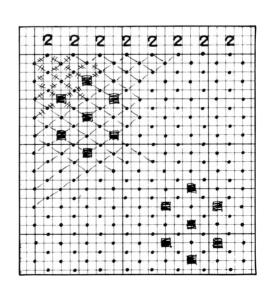

POINT D'ESPRIT IN MECHLIN GROUND

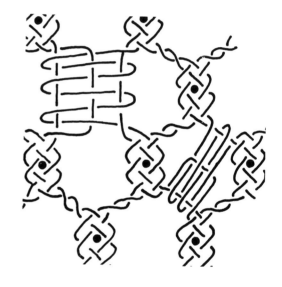

w.s., tw. 1, pin, w.s., tw. 2 at all pinholes
except where tallies indicated

tw. 1, work tallies, tw.1

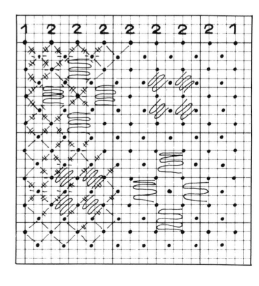

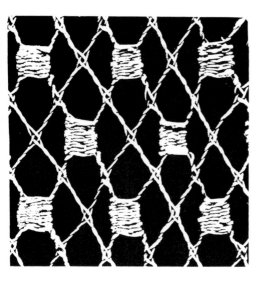

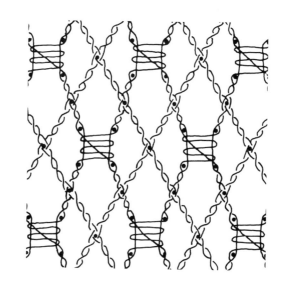

DEVONSHIRE TALLIES NET

diagonals:

    tw. 2 if by a tally, tw. 3 elsewhere

    w.s. with pin in middle at joins

tallies:

    weave squares to fit pricking

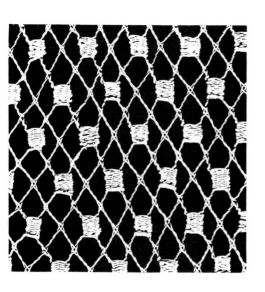

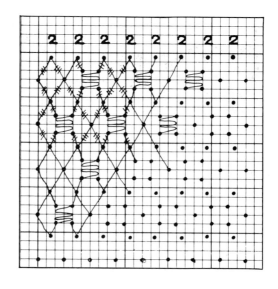

SWING AND A PIN

can only be worked diagonally right to left

prs have to be added at rt hd side as well as at top; then tied out on lt hd side

tw. 3 between diagonal legs

tw. 2 between tallies

tw. 1 between tallies and diagonal joint

diagonal joint: w.s., tw. 3, w.s.

tallies: use far rt hd thread as weaver, weave back and forth ending on far lt hd side

this way the weaver becomes the weaver for the next tally below left, which helps to keep its shape

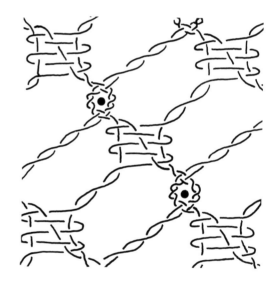

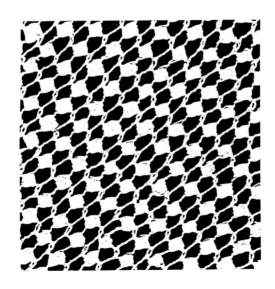

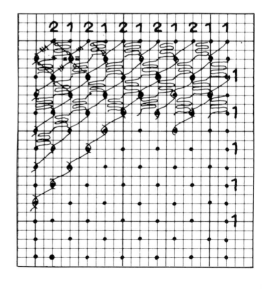

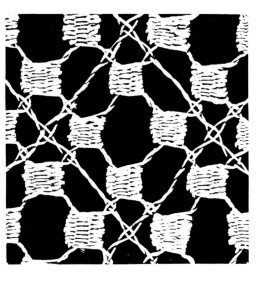

SPOTTED TORCHON GROUND 1

h.s., pin, h.s. throughout

tw. 3 between long distance pinholes
on diagonals

work tallies

tw. 1 after tallies

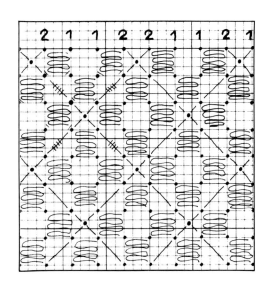

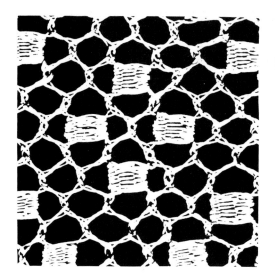

SPOTTED TORCHON GROUND 2

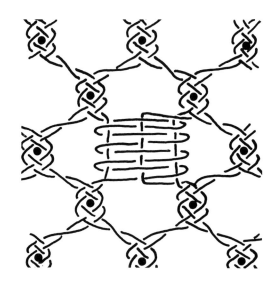

w.s., tw. 1, pin, w.s., tw. 1 throughout

work tallies in pattern as indicated on pricking

tw. 1 after tally

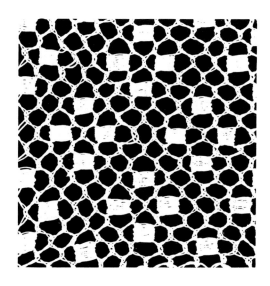

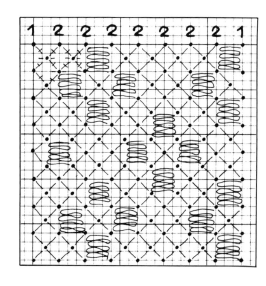

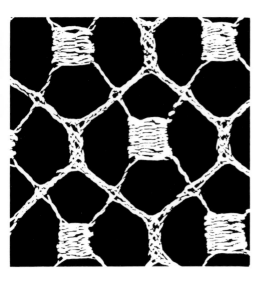

braid x 3½ before and after w.s. group

w.s. group: *w.s. 2 centre prs

w.s. 2 outside prs, pin*

repeat * to * 3 times

w.s. centre prs

diagonals tw. 3 between tallies and braids

w.s. diagonals through braids

tw. 1 before and after tallies

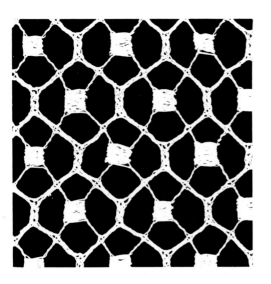

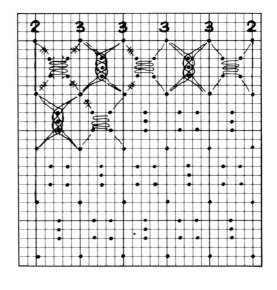

166

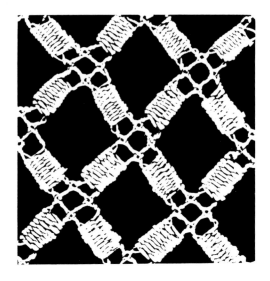

DEVONSHIRE DIAMOND FILLING

work rectangular tallies, pin at bottom
    of each

tw. 3 all prs

w.s., tw. 3 2 centre prs

w.s., tw. 3 2 lt hd prs, pin between prs

w.s., tw. 3 2 rt hd prs, pin between prs

w.s., tw. 3 2 centre prs

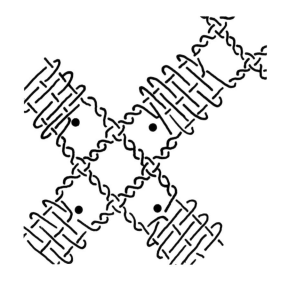

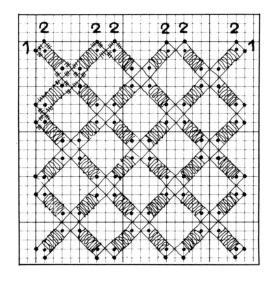

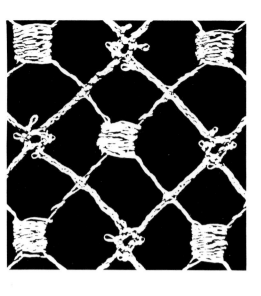

PEARL FILLING WITH TALLIES

work tallies with 2 prs

    tw. 3 before and after
    w.s. through braids at junctions

four pearl filling:
    knotted picot to rt with lt hd braid,
       w.s.
    w.s., tw. 1 2 middle prs
    w.s., 2 rt hd prs picot to rt, w.s.
    w.s., 2 lt hd prs picot to lt, w.s.
    tw. 1, w.s. 2 middle prs
    w.s. 2 rt hd prs picot to lt

braid to next junction

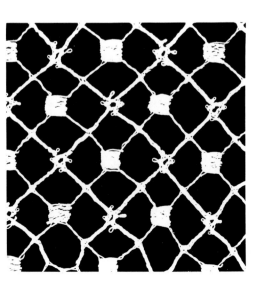

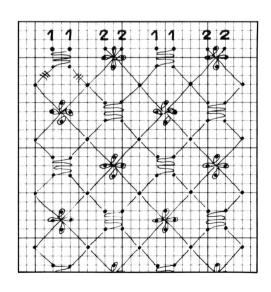

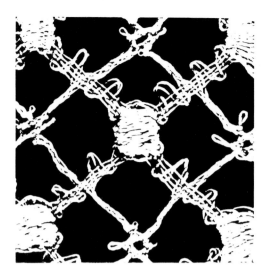

RAISED TALLIES WITH RIBBONS

(2) Devonshire four pearl filling:
   rt hd pr of lt hd braid, picot on rt, w.s.
   2 middle prs — w.s., tw. 1
   2 rt hd prs — w.s., picot to the rt, w.s.
   2 lt hd prs — w.s., picot to the lt, w.s.
   2 middle prs — tw. 1, w.s.
   2 rt hd prs — w.s., picot to the lt

(1) ribbons: w.s. through 2 passive prs, tw. 2
   around winkie pins
   braid: when braid meets passives take lt
   hd pr of braid through and with worker
   pr make new braid, rt hd pr of braid
   work through ribbon
   where braids meet, make a Devonshire
   four pearl filling (see above)
   where ribbons meet, w.s. worker pr with
   adjacent worker pr, tw. 2 both, leave
   with first passive pr from each side pin,
   and make a raised tally
   under tally: w.s. worker prs through next
   passive prs, w.s. these prs to cross them,
   w.s. workers through passive prs again,
   tw. 2 workers, pin, w.s.
   divide workers and continue down ribbons

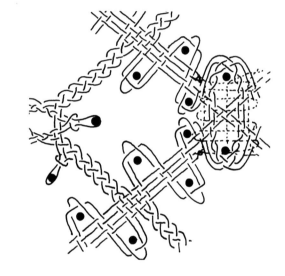

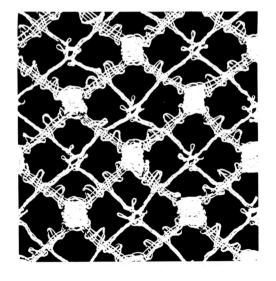

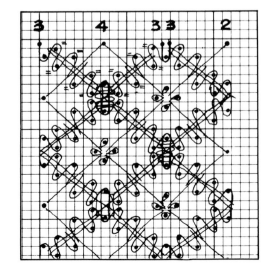

HOLED WALL AND TALLIES

diagonals are made up of 2 sets of 3 prs

*w.s. centre pr with inner pr on both sides
tw. 1, h.s., pin, h.s. inner prs from both
  sides in central pinhole
w.s. these prs back to the opposite outer
  edge through the 2 prs, leave*

repeat * to * once again

place the first 3 prs between tally threads,
  tw. 1, then place second 3 prs between
  tally threads

repeat * to * twice more

lazy join (making sure to keep threads
  in order) where 2 diagonals meet

tw. 3 before and after tallies

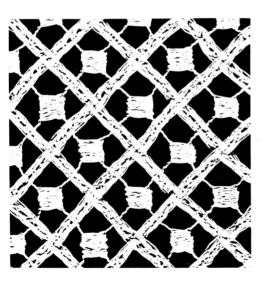

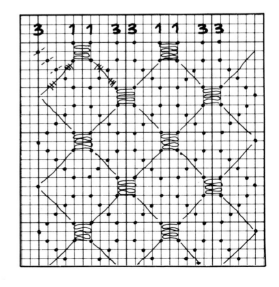

MARGUERITES

w.s., tw. 2, pin, w.s., tw. 2 at all pinholes between flowers

work 4 triangular shaped tallies to centre of flower

w.s. all 4 lt hd prs through 4 rt hd prs

w.s. 2 centre lt prs through lt hd prs

w.s. 2 centre rt prs through rt hd prs

pin

w.s. centre 4 prs through each other

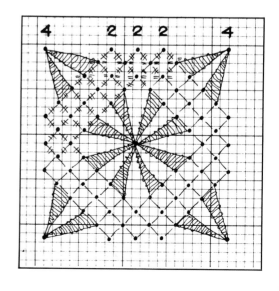

weave long thin leaves

w.s. centre through each other

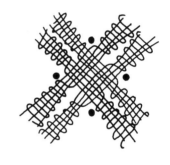

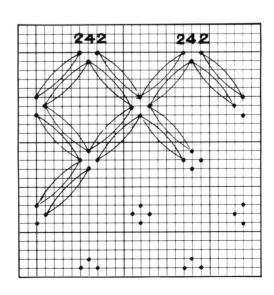

MARGUERITES IN FRAME

the horizontal prs work lt to rt one row, then reverse the next row

tw. 2, w.s., tw. 2 horizontal and vertical prs

work leaves to flower centres

pin between all prs

w.s. centre 4 prs through each other

w.s. bottom pr from leaf through 2 prs to centre, leave (both sides)

w.s. horizontal prs through 3 prs, w.s. 2 horizontal prs through each other, then w.s. through next 3 prs

w.s. 2 centre prs out through 2 prs to outside edge

w.s. all next 4 prs through each other

pin before continuing

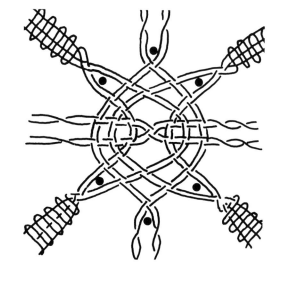

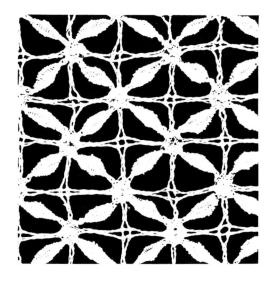

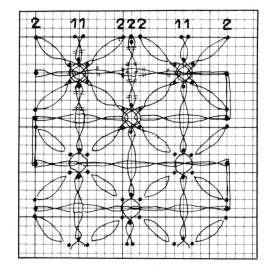

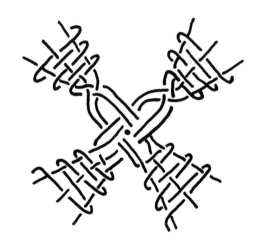

weave flat leaves as shown

lazy join between each 4 leaf joint

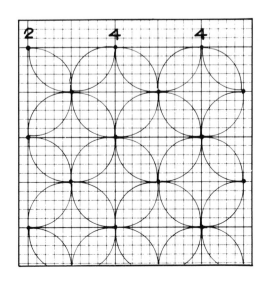

w.s. each start of leaf

at join, use bobbins in prs instead of
singly, w.s. with pin in middle

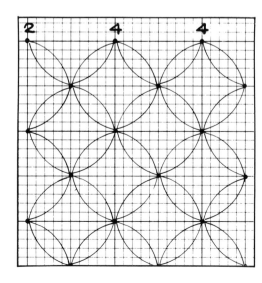

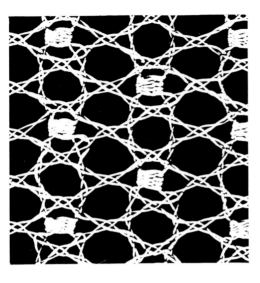

KAT STITCH
WITH TALLIES

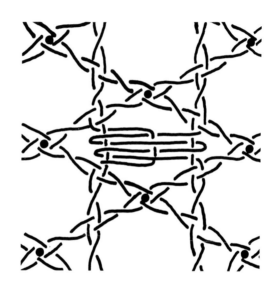

h.s., pin, h.s.

w.s., tw. 1 at intersections

work tallies where indicated

tw. 1 both prs at bottom of tallies

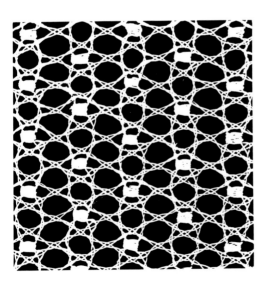

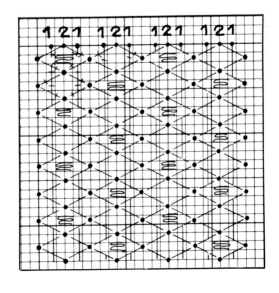

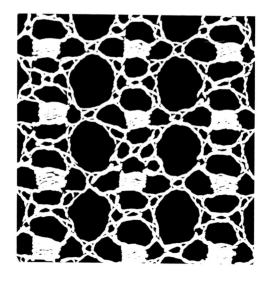

HONEYCOMB WITH TALLIES INSIDE

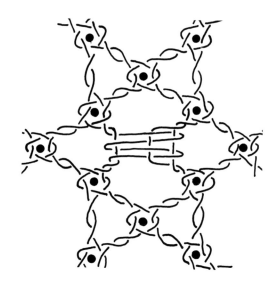

work honeycomb st. throughout:
 h.s., tw. 1, pin, h.s., tw. 1

work tallies as indicated:
 tw. 1 before tallies,
 tw. 2 after tallies

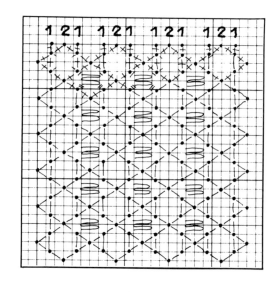

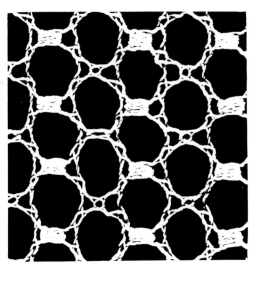

HONEYCOMB
WITH TALLIES

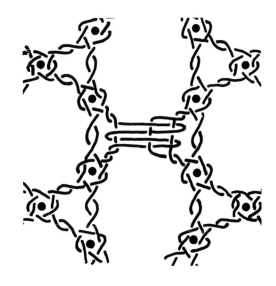

work honeycomb st. throughout:
    h.s., tw. 1, pin, h.s., tw. 1

work tallies as indicated:
    tw. 1 before tallies
    tw. 2 after tallies

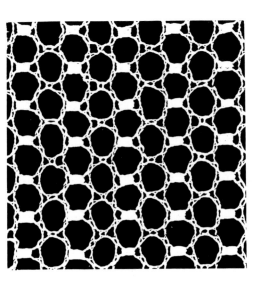

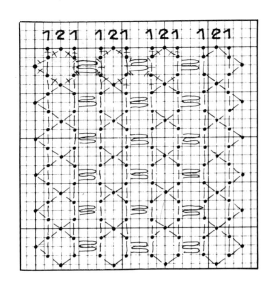

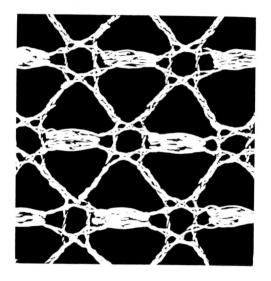

STAR CROSSING WITH TALLIES

tw. 2, w.s., tw. 2 between crossings

w.s., tw. 1 both diagonals at top of crossings

w.s., tw. 1 centre 2 prs, then w.s., tw. 1 back through vertical prs

make wide shallow tally with pr from adjacent crossing, tw. 1 both prs

w.s., tw. 1 pr from tally through vertical pr both sides

w.s., tw. 1 centre 2 prs

w.s. 2 outside prs that become next diagonals

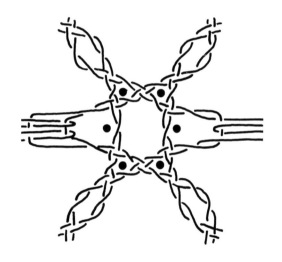

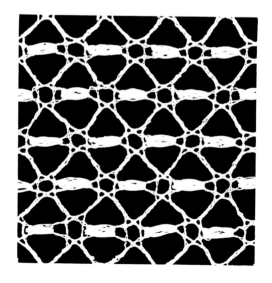

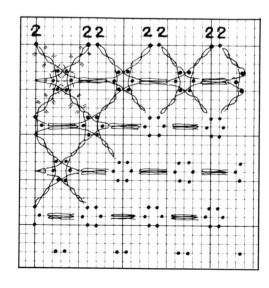

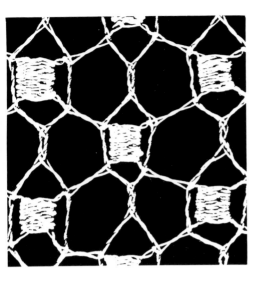

tw. 2, work tallies, tw. 2

tw. 3 verticals to lt and rt of tallies only

tw. 2 elsewhere

w.s., pin, tw. 2, w.s., tw. 2 at intersection
     between tallies

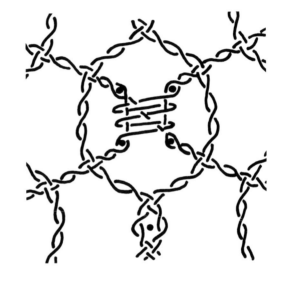

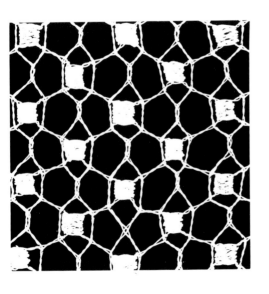

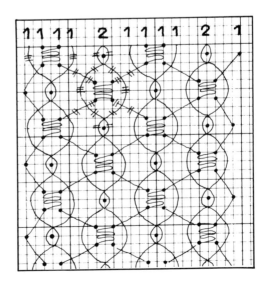

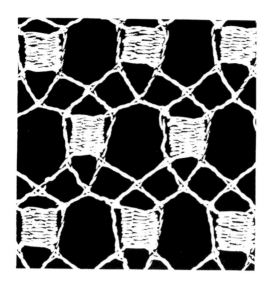

TALLIES AND LATTICE

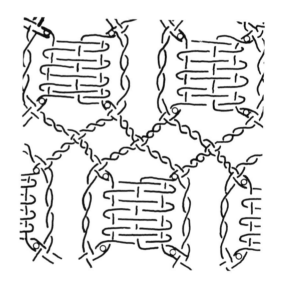

w.s. 2 lt hd prs and 2 rt hd prs at top of tallies

tw. 3 the 2 outside prs

tw. 1, then make tally with 2 inner prs

w.s., tw. 3 lattice band between tally rows

should be made with no pins, but when a large area is to be filled, it is best to use temporary pins at top and bottom of tallies and remove pins as soon as possible

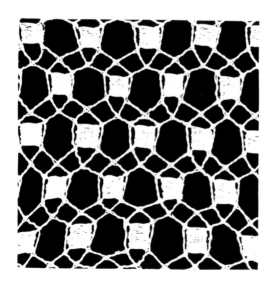

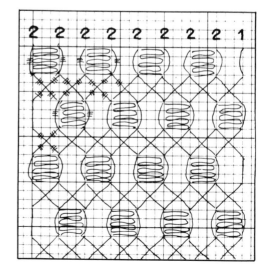

HERRINGBONE

work left to right, then right to left
    throughout

work tally, the weaver always starts and
    finishes on rt hd side on the left to right
    row and reversed on next row

tw. 1, pin, tw. 2, pin, tw. 1 at all junctions

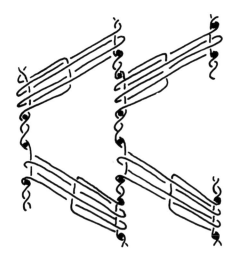

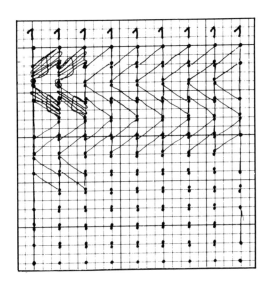

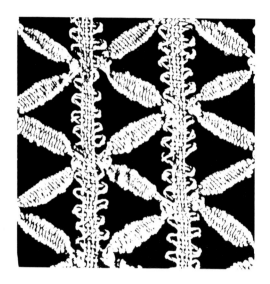

DEVONSHIRE BARS AND TALLIES

w.s. trails with tw. 2 round winkie pin

weave narrow leaves, w.s. workers through,
 pin, w.s. back

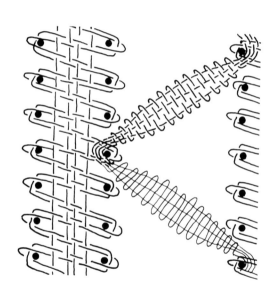

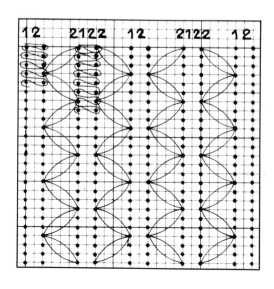

DEVONSHIRE TALLIES AND HORIZONTALS

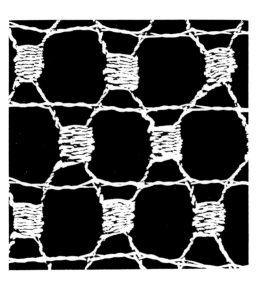

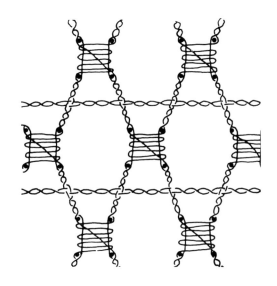

horizontals and diagonals:
   tw. 3, w.s., tw. 3

tallies:
   pin between prs to start

   knot after weaving, push knot close to
   work with pin

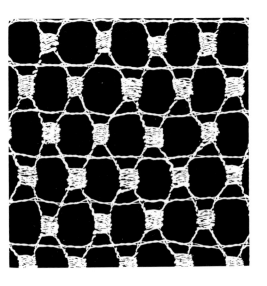

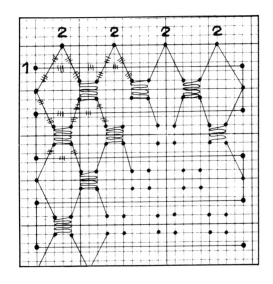

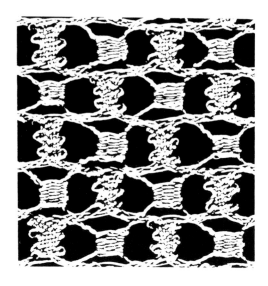

DEVONSHIRE
TOAD IN THE HOLE

bottom left of brick after last passive has
been worked: w.s. tally diagonal pr
through both brick prs

w.s. brick prs again

bottom right of brick, w.s. passives, w.s.
tally diagonal through both prs, w.s.
passives again

tallies diagonal: tw. 3 before and after
tallies

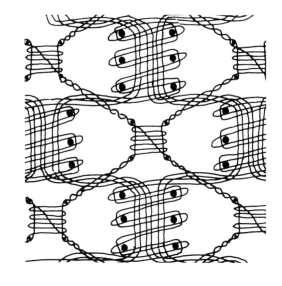

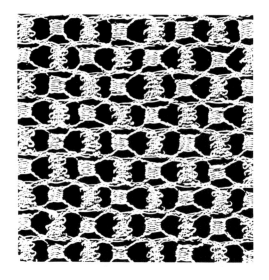

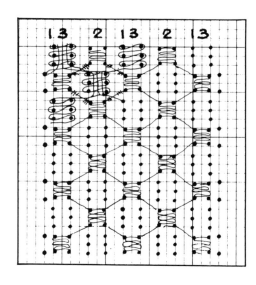

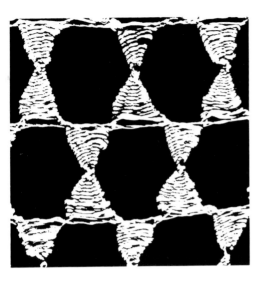

when horizontals meet prs from triangular
    tallies: w.s. with pin in middle

tw. 3 horizontals between pins

w.s., pin, w.s. at middle junction of
    tallies

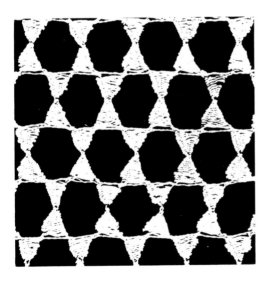

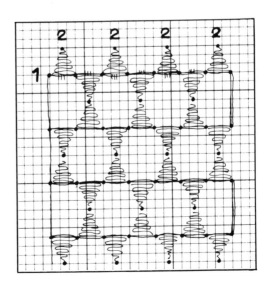

HOURGLASS TALLIES WITH DIAGONALS

w.s. with pin in middle at junction of diagonals with triangular tallies

where diagonals meet horizontals, w.s. diagonals first, then w.s. through both prs, pin between to support

tw. 3 all horizontal and vertical prs between junctions

w.s. at base of triangle, w.s. horizontal through these prs using each vertical pr as one

w.s. at top of next triangle

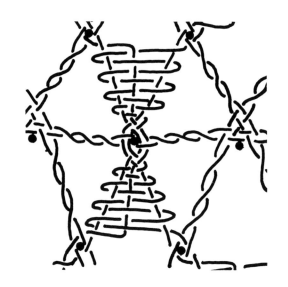

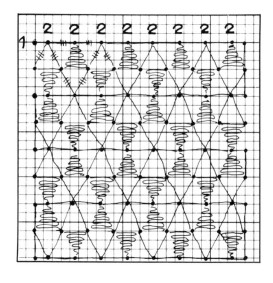

TULIPS

w.s., tw. 2 lattice work between tulips

weave top threads as usual until pin on
   rt, weave worker through 2 threads
   from lattice band, pin

weave to left under 1st thread, over next
   2 threads, under next thread, over next
   2 threads, and under last thread, (having
   brought in corresponding pr from
   lattice work above)

work back and forth thus using single
   and double threads until the bottom
   of tulip

w.s. 4 central threads
w.s. 2 lt hd prs
w.s. 2 rt hd prs

place temporary pins to hold shape

braid until next tulip

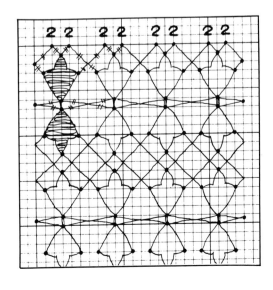

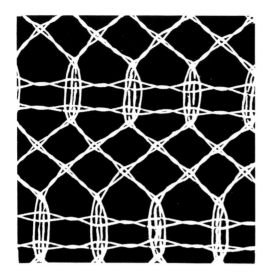

FISH WITH TWO HORIZONTALS 1

w.s., pin at top of fish

w.s. horizontal bars through fish

tw. 2 horizontal bars between fish

pin, w.s., tw. 2 at bottom of fish

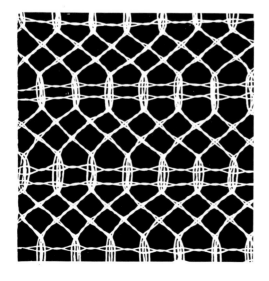

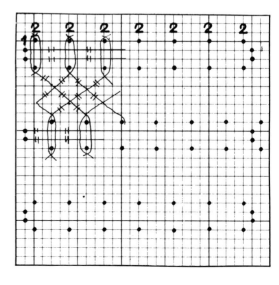

FISH WITH TWO HORIZONTALS 2

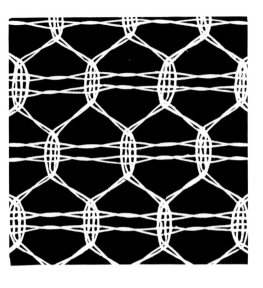

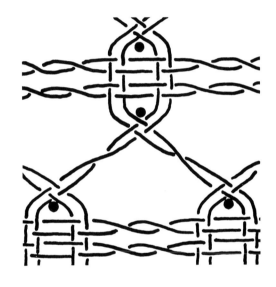

tw. 1 diag. lines

w.s., pin

w.s. horizontal bars through fish

tw. 2 between fish

pin, w.s. at bottom of fish

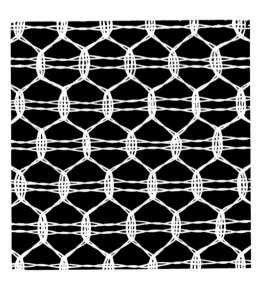

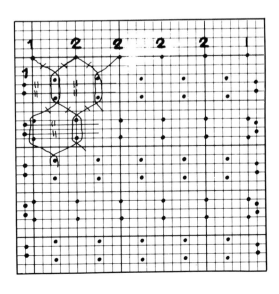

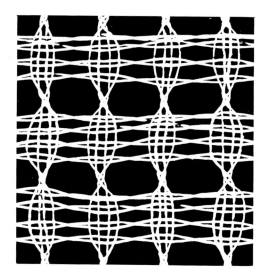

FISH WITH FOUR HORIZONTALS 1

pin and tw. 1 vertical fish prs

w.s., pin and tw. 1

w.s. through all horizontal prs

tw. 1 horizontal prs between fish

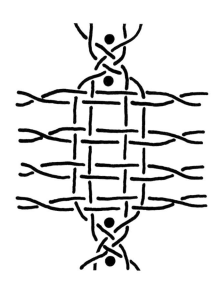

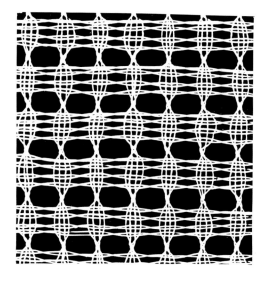

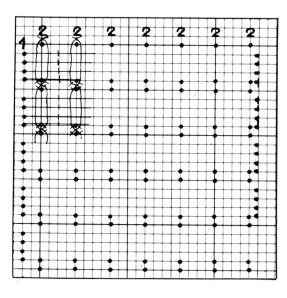

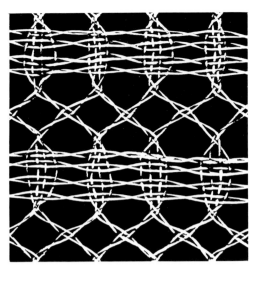

FISH WITH FOUR HORIZONTALS 2

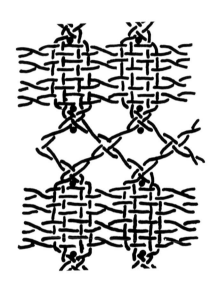

top of fish: w.s., tw. 1, pin, start
  horizontals at top, support with pin

w.s. through fish, tw. 1 between

bottom of fish: pin, tw. 1, w.s., pin, tw. 1

w.s., tw. 1 diagonal lines

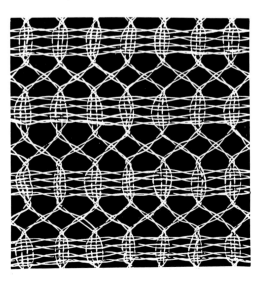

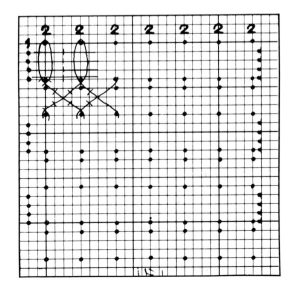

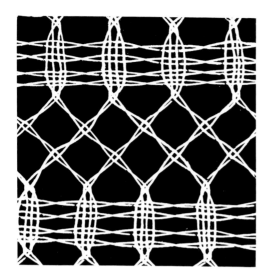

FISH WITH FOUR HORIZONTALS 3

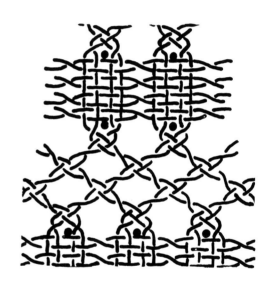

top and bottom of fish:
  tw. 1, w.s., pin, tw. 1

w.s. horizontals through vertical fish

tw. 1 all 4 horizontals between fish

w.s., tw. 1 lattice work between fish

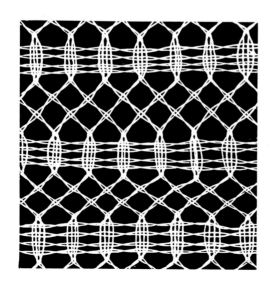

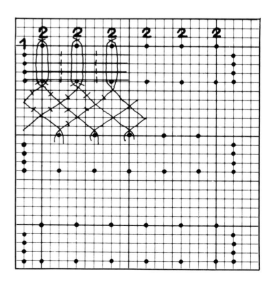

DOUBLE FISH

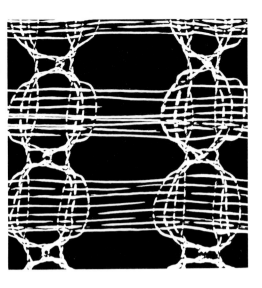

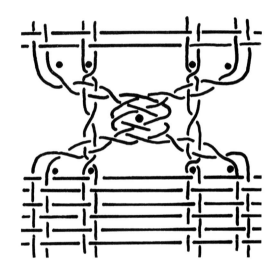

pin at top and bottom of fish to hold
   verticals open and in place

no tw. on horizontals

w.s., pin, tw. 1, w.s. between fish

all other joints w.s.

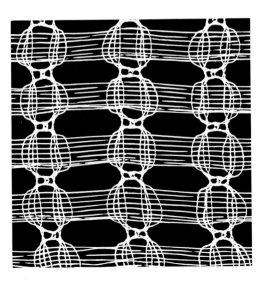

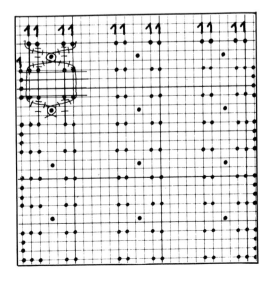

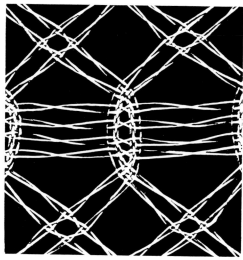

ITALIAN FISH

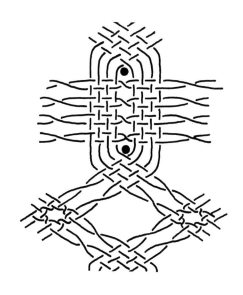

w.s. 4 legs through each other

pin

tw. 1 horizontals in and between fish

pin

w.s. 4 legs through again

tw. 1 diagonals between joints, w.s.,
   tw. 1, w.s. at joint

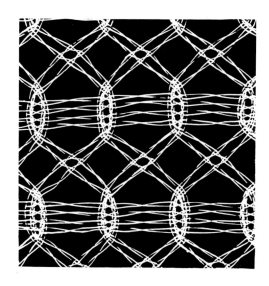

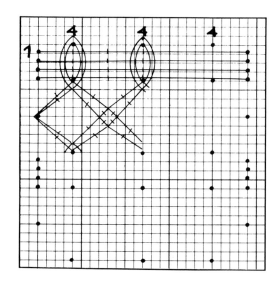

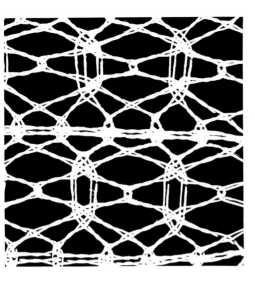

ITALIAN SPIDER VARIATION

w.s., tw. 2 all diagonals where two meet

w.s., tw. 1, pin, w.s., tw. 2 at pinhole
between spiders

pin as indicated top and bottom of spider

junction with horizontal bars:
    w.s. 2 diagonal prs
    w.s. horizontal prs through diagonal prs
    w.s. 2 diagonal prs again
    tw. 2 diagonals and horizontals

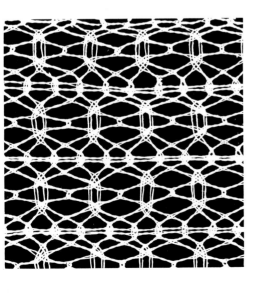

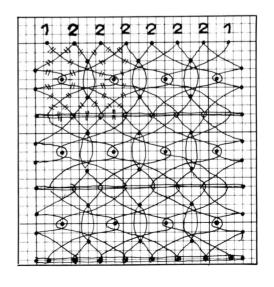

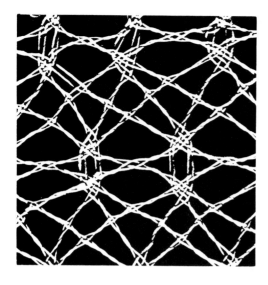

ITALIAN SPIDER WITH EYE

tw. 2 all diagonals

w.s. where two meet

w.s. with pin in middle at all pinholes

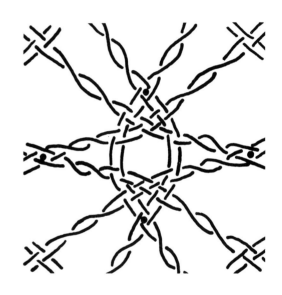

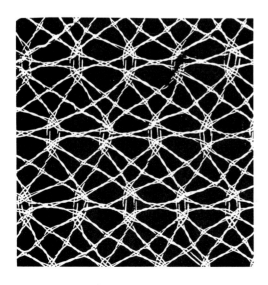

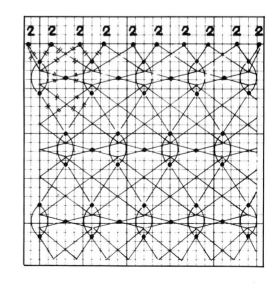

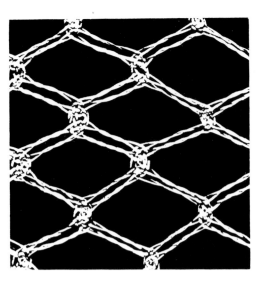

SPIDER WITH TWO LEGS

tw. 3 all diagonals
normal w.s. spider

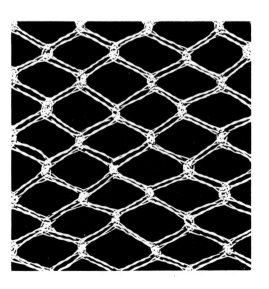

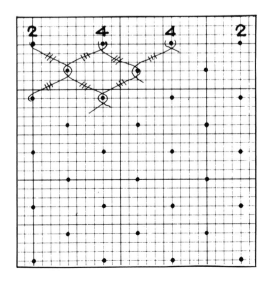

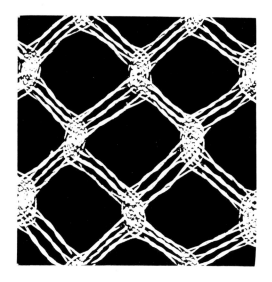

PLAIN TORCHON SPIDERS

tw. 3 all legs

w.s. all lt hd prs through rt hd prs

pin

w.s. all rt hd prs through lt hd prs

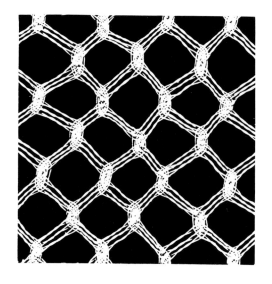

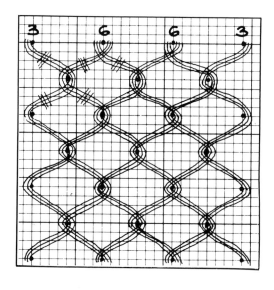

SPIDER WITH TORCHON GROUND

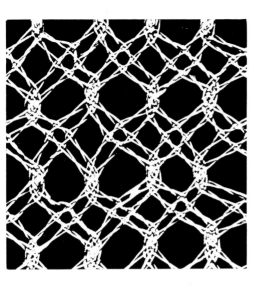

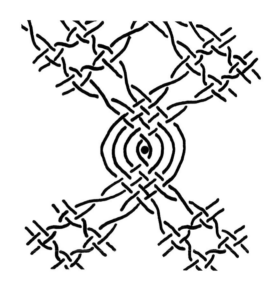

work spider as normal

one tw. between w.s. joints

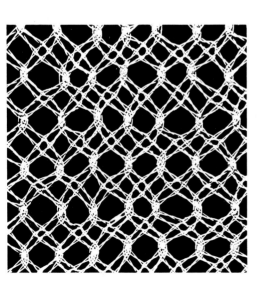

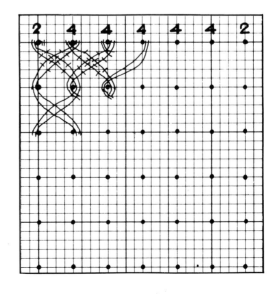

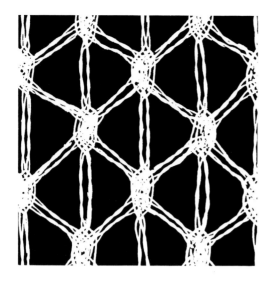

SPIDER WITH VERTICALS

This spider is also sometimes called Petits Pois de Dieppe.

tw. 3 each leg

pin and w.s. at top of spider

pin in middle of spider

pin after last w.s.

tw. 3 all legs

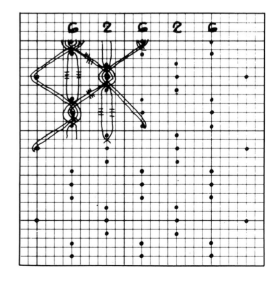

EYELESS SPIDER

This spider is also sometimes called Fond de Neige.

tw. 2 diagonal legs

tw. 3 vertical legs

pin at top of spider to retain shape

w.s. throughout

w.s. through bottom vert. prs, pin

tw. 2 all 6 prs

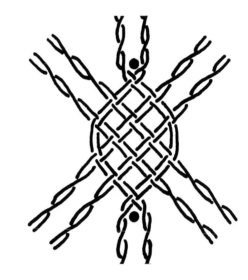

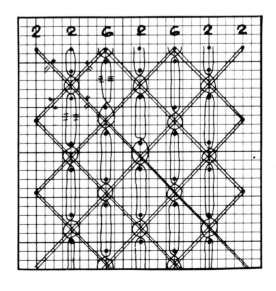

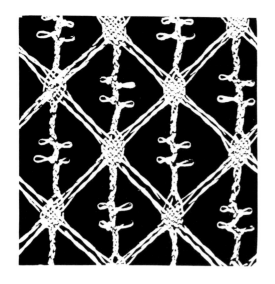

EYELESS SPIDER WITH PICOTS

tw. 3 diagonal legs

braid verticals until picots

work knotted picots with h.s. between

braid x 4

work knotted picots with h.s. between

braid until start of spider, pin between
   prs

work eyeless spider

pin before start of next braid

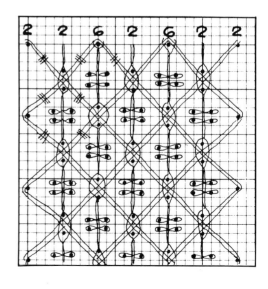

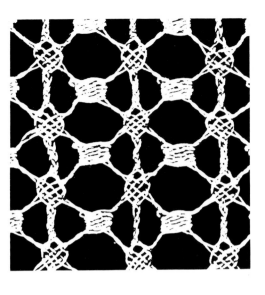

SIMPLE SPIDER
AND TALLIES

braid between spiders

pin before and after braid

tw. 2 before and after tallies

w.s. with no twists throughout spider

pin at sides to keep shape

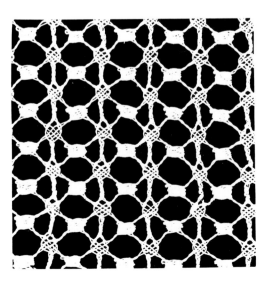

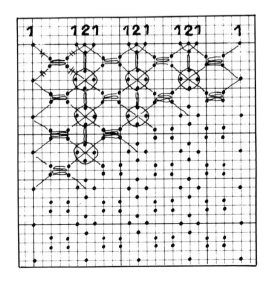

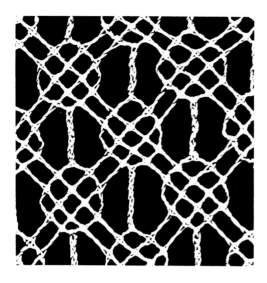

TWISTED SPIDER AND BRAID

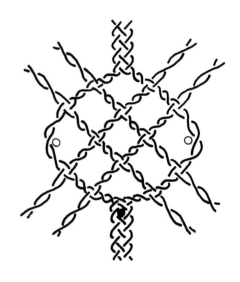

braid to top of spider

tw. 2 legs between spiders

w.s., tw. 2 throughout except far rt and
    lt of outer circle — tw. 3

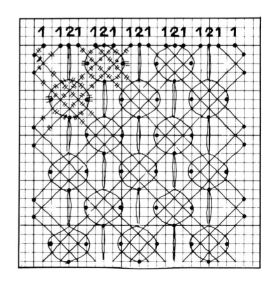

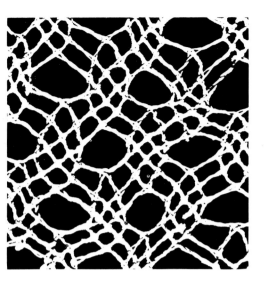

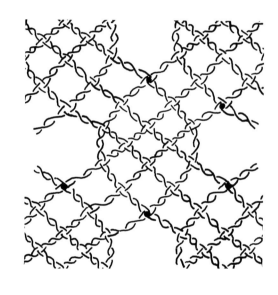

w.s., tw. 2 throughout

pin in middle of top and bottom w.s.

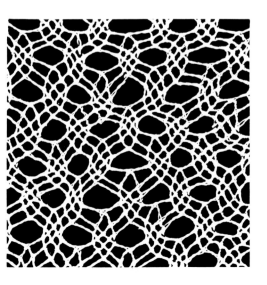

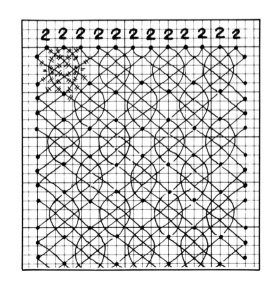

SPIDER'S EYE

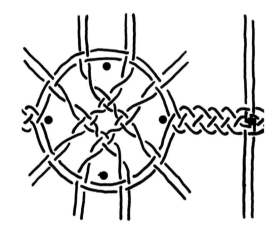

work horizontally only

braid to circle, pin and divide

w.s. top pr through diagonals and
    verticals

tw. 1 all 4 prs

w.s., tw. 1 2 centre prs
w.s., tw. 1 2 lt hd prs
w.s., tw. 1 2 rt hd prs
w.s., tw. 1 2 centre prs

w.s. bottom circumference pr through
    these 4 prs

pin before starting braiding

w.s. verticals through braid pin in middle
    to support

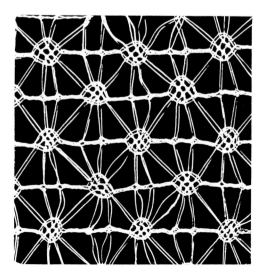

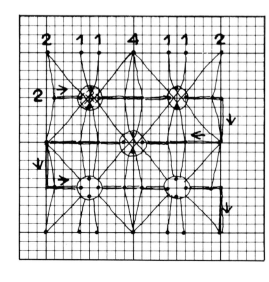

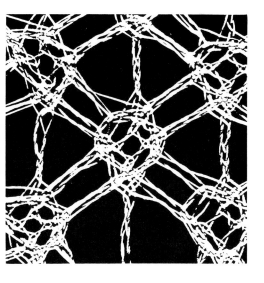

PHEASANT'S EYE

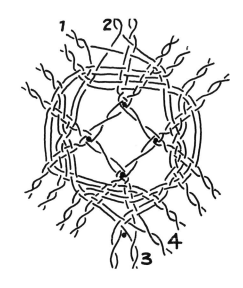

cross 2 centre threads from 1 and 2 and
w.s. rt hd pr through 2 prs as diagram

w.s. all other legs, as diagram

note: tw. 1 legs in inner circle before
h.s., pin, h.s.

note: at base of eye, divide prs 3 and 4
before twisting

vertical legs, tw. 2, h.s., pin, h.s., tw. 1
all other legs, tw. 2

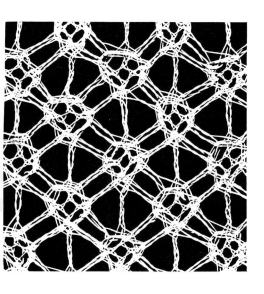

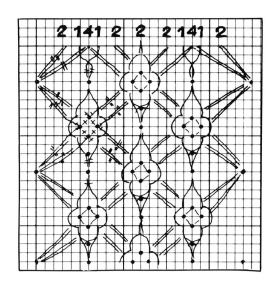

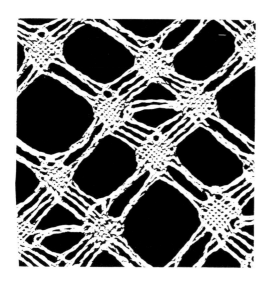

CLOVER

buds are in groups of four

tw. 2 all legs between buds in each group

tw. 2, braid x 3, tw. 2 outer legs between each group

w.s., pin, central prs
w.s., tw. 1 outer prs through legs
w.s. 6 inner prs through each other
w.s. top rt hd pr through outer pr, tw. 2, w.s. through outer pr of adjacent bud, tw. 1, pin, w.s. back through outer pr, tw. 2, w.s. through original outer pr, pin, tw. 1, w.s. out again

w.s., tw. 1 outer prs through rest of central prs

pin and w.s.

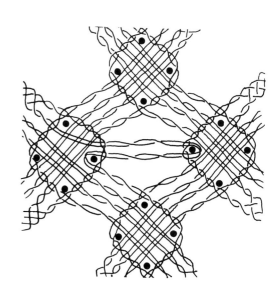

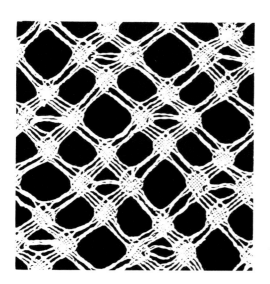

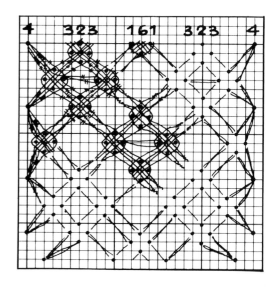

ROUND SPIDER

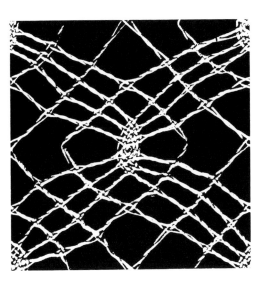

tw. 3 legs of spider

tw. 2 between each other point

w.s. with pin in middle at all pinholes
except spider centres and shapers each
side of spiders

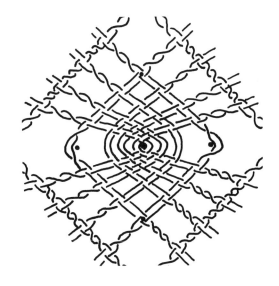

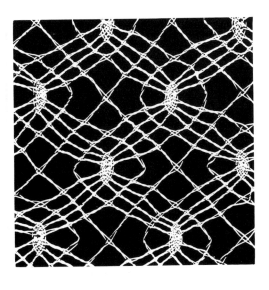

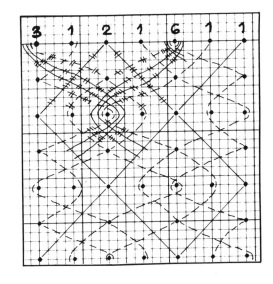

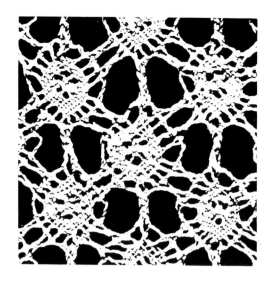

HALOED SPIDER

tw. 2, w.s., tw. 2 all legs

braid using each pr as single threads, all
    verticals between buds

pin, w.s. 2 inside prs round pin, tw. 2
    all 4 prs

the inner prs become outside circumference
    prs which w.s., tw. 2 through all legs,
    tw. 2 all legs again

w.s. spider as diagram

note: tw. 3 centre 4 legs before w.s. centre
    and tw. 3 again

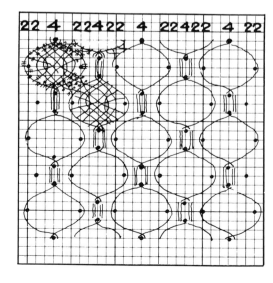

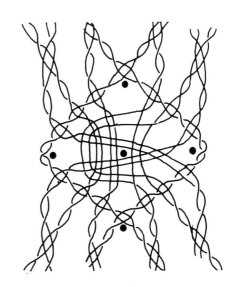

BINCHE SPIDERS

211

Binche spiders are also sometimes called Point de Flandres, Round Spiders, or Open-Eyed Spiders.

tw. 2 diagonals
   w.s. through each other, tw. 2

tw. 1 legs and outer circle between
   joins *except* at side pins, tw. 3

w.s. throughout

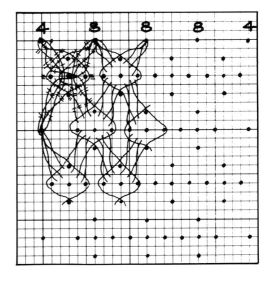

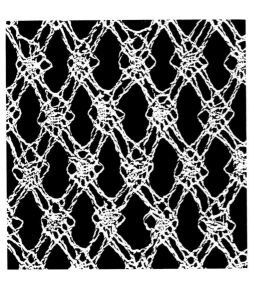

DAISY SPIDER

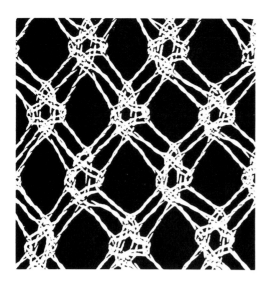

w.s. at top of spider

w.s. next 2 prs through spider passives
and then through each other

w.s. back out of spider on the opposite
side

w.s. through next 2 prs, pin, w.s., tw. 1
at winkie pin

return through spider passives

w.s. through each other in centre

w.s. out through spider passives on
opposite side

pin and w.s. base of spider

tw. 3 all 6 legs before starting next spider

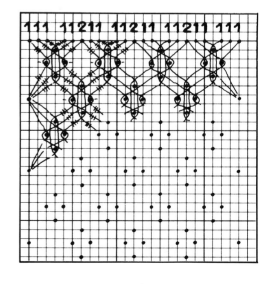

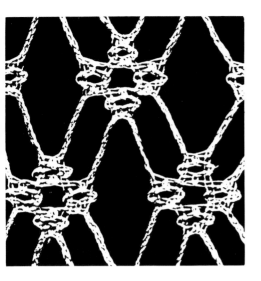

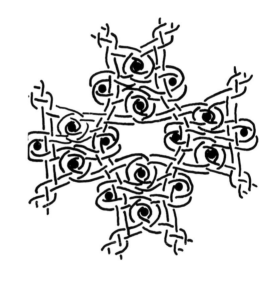

braid legs until spider

w.s., pin, w.s. top pinhole

w.s., tw. 1 outside pr, w.s. with new prs at next lt and rt pinholes

w.s., pin, w.s. at bottom pinhole

braid to next spider

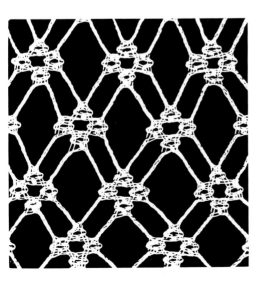

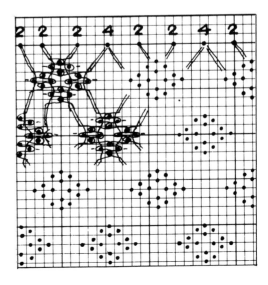

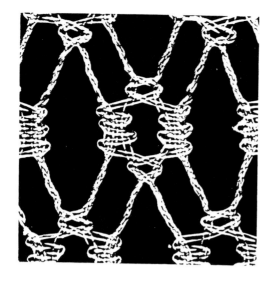

LARGE ROSE GROUND SPIDER

braid legs until spider
w.s. throughout
tw. 1 at winkie pins

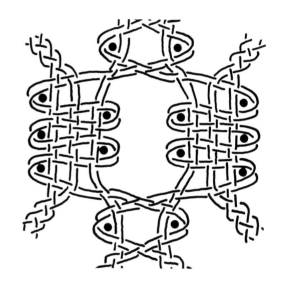

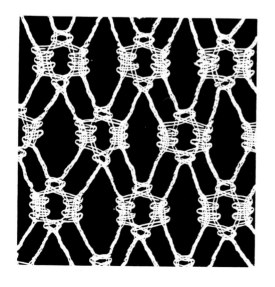

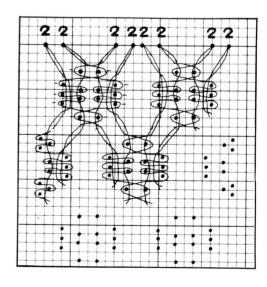

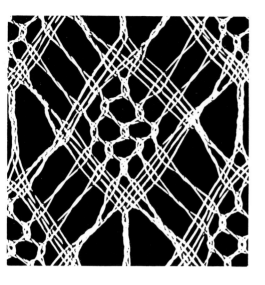

w.s. 4 passives through each other at top of diamond

w.s. all 6 legs through passives, tw. 1

w.s., pin, w.s., tw. 1 all mini spiders in order (as diagram)

w.s. legs out through passives

w.s. all 4 passives through each other, pin at base of diamond

tw. 2, pin, braid x 4, tw. 2 at A, B, C and D

braid with bottom middle 2 prs until top of next diamond

tw. 3 remaining legs both sides

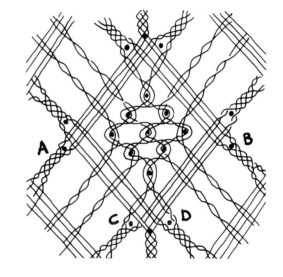

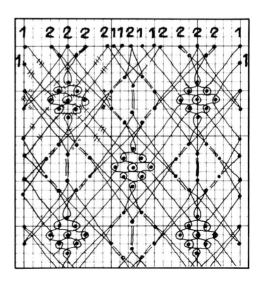

PEASANT SPIDERS 2

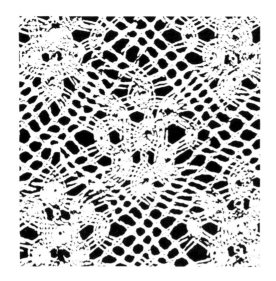

frame:
> w.s., tw. 1 throughout (legs leaving frame are untwisted)

work mini spiders as diagram from the top

note: prs from 1 w.s. through each other, then they become the outside pr of first spider, w.s. through each other at base of first spider and w.s. back through each other before circling middle spider, repeat again before circling bottom spider

note: passive prs 4 and 5 w.s. through legs in turn, and are not part of any spider

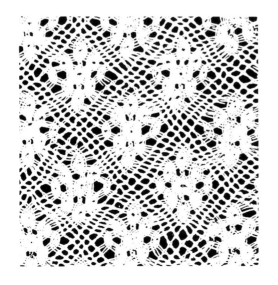

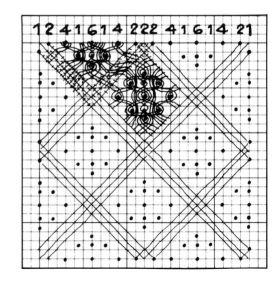

BINCHE SPIDERS IN DOUBLE TULLE

This is also sometimes called Eyeless Spider.

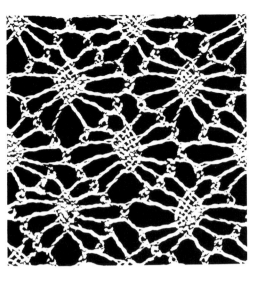

tw. 3 all legs

circumference pr encircles w.s. cross-
over spider

diagonal lines: w.s., pin, tw. 2, w.s., tw. 2

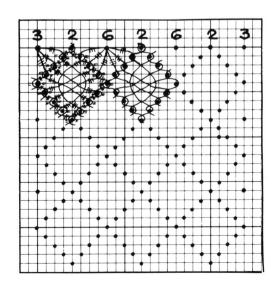

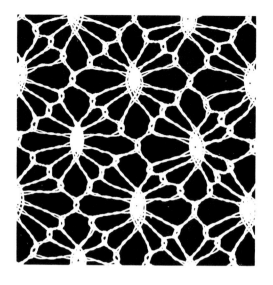

SPIDERS IN DOUBLE TULLE

tw. 3 all legs

w.s. spider with pin in middle

tw. 3 all legs

diag. lines: w.s., pin, tw. 2, w.s., tw. 2

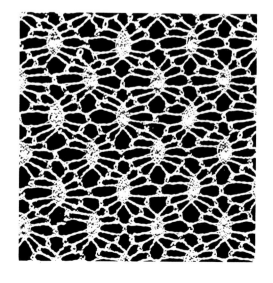

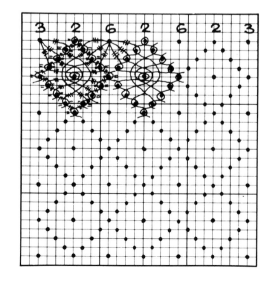

SPIDERS IN HALF STITCH DIAGONALS

h.s. back and forth diagonals picking up legs one side and leaving out prs the other

junction of diagonals:
  h.s., pin, h.s. 2 centre prs at top of pinhole diamond
  h.s., pin, h.s. 2 lt hd prs and 2 rt hd prs
  h.s., pin, h.s. 2 centre prs
  tw. 1 all legs before spider and tw. 2 after

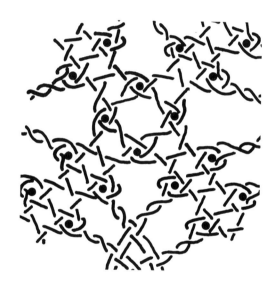

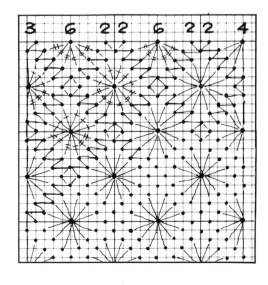

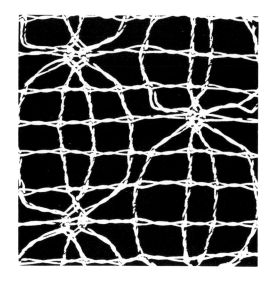

top of cage:
   w.s. 2 lt hd prs, tw. 2 lt hd pr
   w.s. 2 rt hd prs, tw. 2 rt hd pr
   pin both sides to keep shape
   w.s., tw. 2 horizontal and vertical prs,
   horizontal pr goes back and forth as
   indicated
   w.s. 2 centre prs
   pin both sides
   w.s. 2 lt hd prs
   w.s. 2 rt hd prs
   w.s. horizontals through all 4 prs

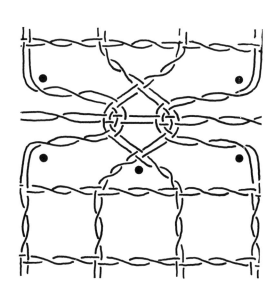

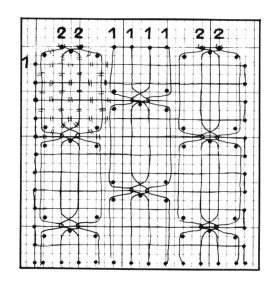

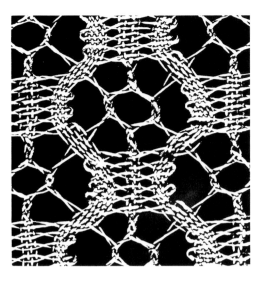

ITALIAN SPIDER WITH RIBBONS

spiders:
    vertical legs w.s., tw. 1, pin
    w.s., tw. 1 diagonal legs, tw.1, w.s.,
    tw. 1, pin, w.s., tw. 1

w.s. throughout remainder with tw. 2 at
    winkie pins

note: 3 prs in ribbon on left of spider and
    4 prs on right

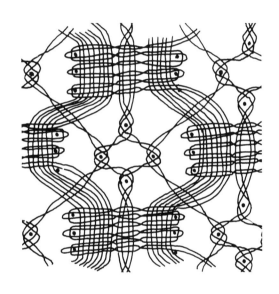

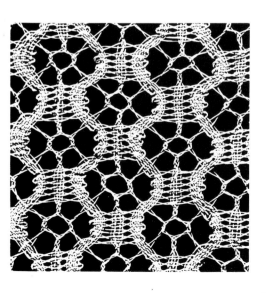

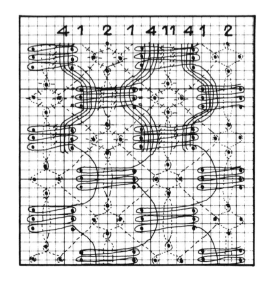

RIBBON BEADING 1

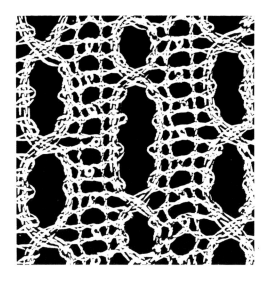

w.s. throughout

w.s., tw. 1 before and after tramlines

w.s., pin, w.s. between tramlines

tw. 2 at winkie pins

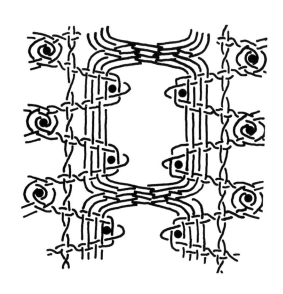

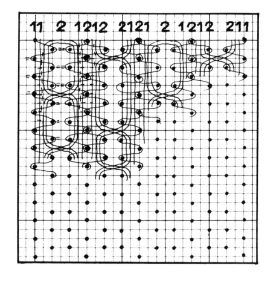

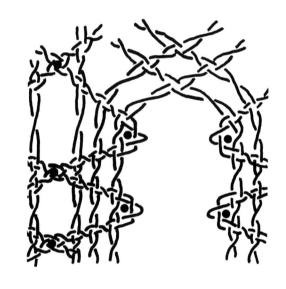

w.s., tw. 1, throughout

tw. 1 at winkie pins

h.s., pin, h.s. between vertical lines

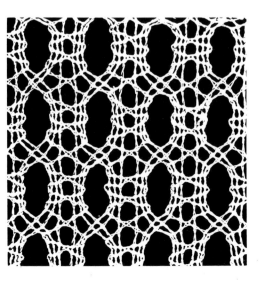

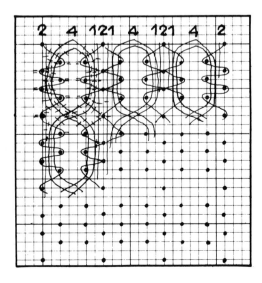

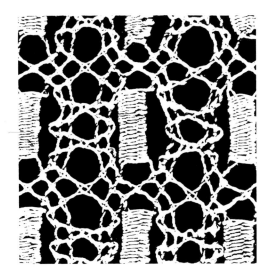

RIBBON BEADING WITH TALLIES

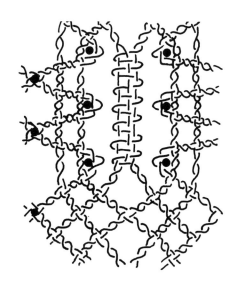

w.s., tw. 2 at each joint

h.s., pin, h.s., tw. 2 at joints between
  spiders

tw. 2 at winkie pins

tw. 2 all prs before and after tallies

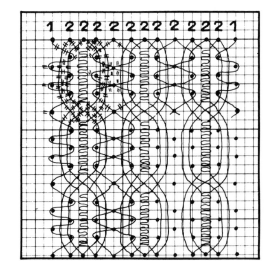

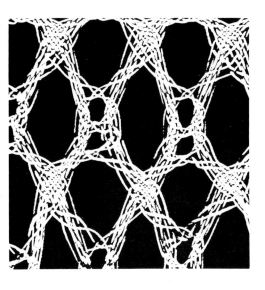

top of spider:
    w.s. all 8 prs through each other
    put pin each side of centre 2 prs
        centre 2 prs — w.s. through passives

figure of eight join:
    with corresponding worker from next
    motif tw. 1 both prs, h.s., pin, h.s.

    *w.s. through passives either side, leave
    w.s. pr. last worked back through
        passives — both sides

    tw.1, h.s., pin, h.s. *

    repeat from * to * once more

    w.s. through passives either side

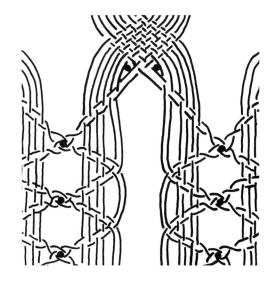

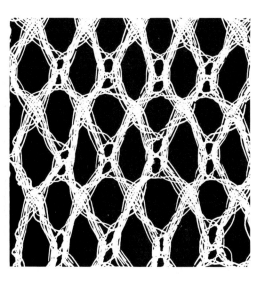

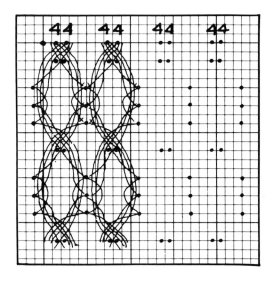

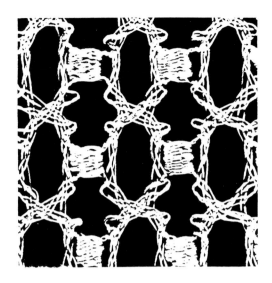

*lt side: first pr tw. 3, make tally with
    adjacent pr, tw. 3 each leg of tally
w.s. next 2 prs beside tally
w.s. pr nearest tally with tally leg, tw. 2
    round winkie pin, leave
w.s. leg and 3rd pr then w.s. worker
    through both prs*
repeat from * to * on rt hd side
w.s. centre 2 prs
w.s. these prs out to lt through 2 prs
repeat on rt side
w.s. centre 2 prs
*w.s. these prs out to lt through 2 prs,
    tw. 2 round winkie pin
w.s. worker pr through 2 prs
w.s. 2 lt hd prs, tw. 3 lt hd pr before
    making tally
repeat from * to * on rt hd side

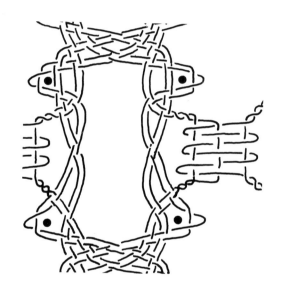

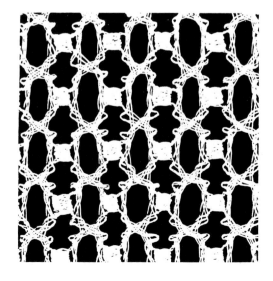

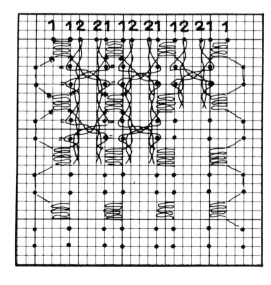

DIAGONAL RIBBONS

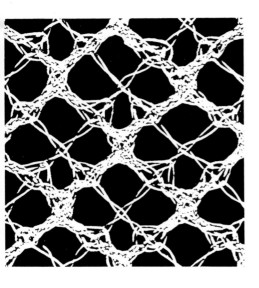

diagonals:
   h.s., pin, h.s., w.s. through legs (tw. 1 diagonals only)

legs before spider:
   lt leg — w.s. lt hd pr with next 2 prs, twice
   rt leg — w.s. rt hd pr with next 2 prs, twice

spider:
   *w.s. centre prs
   w.s. centre lt with 2 prs to lt
   w.s. centre rt with 2 prs to rt
   repeat from * once more
   w.s. centre lt with 1 pr to lt
   w.s. centre rt with 1 pr to rt
   w.s. centre prs

legs after spider:
   as before but reversed

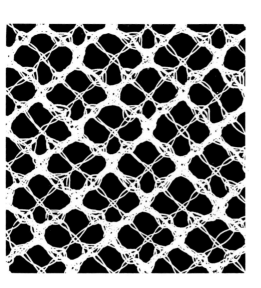

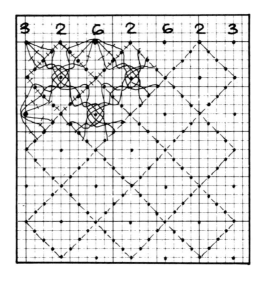

TORCHON STAR

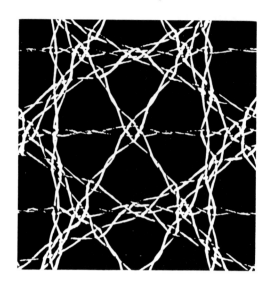

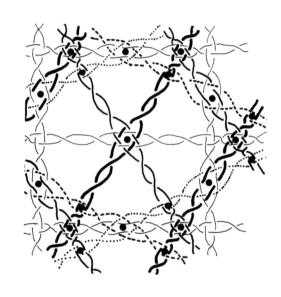

tw. 2 round big star

tw. 1 each other pair

pin in centre of 3 pr cross

w.s. where 2 prs cross

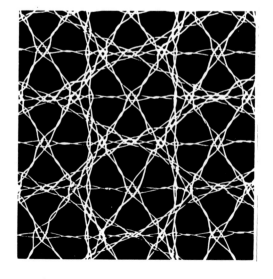

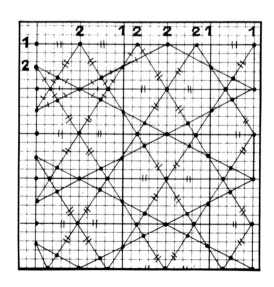

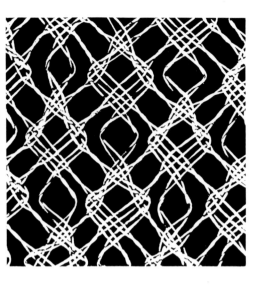

tw. 2 all legs

w.s. 1 through 2 and 3
w.s. 4 through 2 and 3

w.s. prs from 1 and 4
w.s. prs from 2 and 3

w.s. 5 through 4 and 1
w.s. 6 through 3 and 2

w.s. pr from 4 through 1
w.s. pr from 3 through 2

w.s. 5 through 6 and pr from 3
w.s. pr from 4 through 6 and pr from 3

tw. 2 all legs

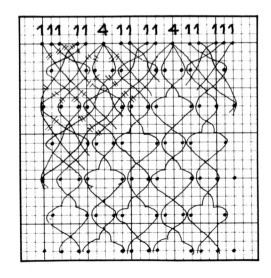

BUD STAR 2

w.s. 1 through 2 and 3
w.s. 4 through 2 and 3

w.s. prs from 1 and 4
w.s. prs from 2 and 3

w.s. 5 through 4 and 1
w.s. 6 through 3 and 2

w.s. pr from 4 through 1
w.s. pr from 3 through 2

tw. 1 prs from 5 and 6

w.s. 5 through 6 and pr from 3
w.s. pr from 4 through 6 and pr from 3

tw. 4 vertical legs, pin to separate them

tw. 2 all other legs

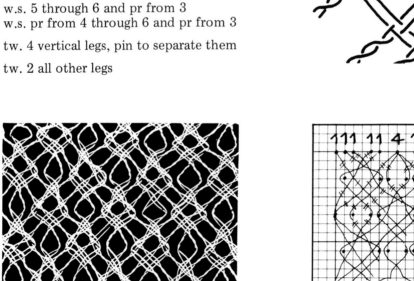

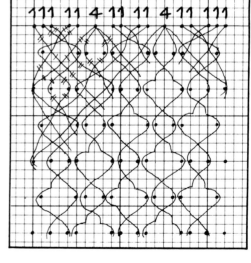

BUD STAR 3

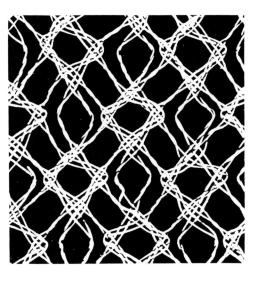

tw. 4 vertical legs, pin to separate them

w.s. 1 through 2 and 3
w.s. 4 through 2 and 3

w.s. prs from 1 and 4
w.s. prs from 2 and 3

w.s. 5 through 4 and 1
w.s. 6 through 3 and 2

w.s. pr from 4 through 1 and 5
w.s. pr from 3 through 2 and 6

w.s. pr from 4 through 3 and 6
w.s. pr from 5 through 3 and 6

tw. 4 vertical legs

tw. 2 other legs

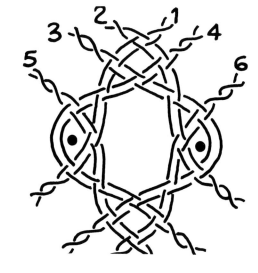

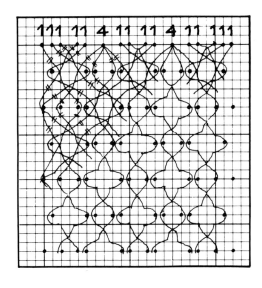

BUD STAR 4

w.s. 1 and 2 through 3 and 4

tw. 1 prs from 2 and 4

w.s. 5 through 1 and 2

w.s. 6 through 3 and 4

w.s. 1 and 2 also 3 and 4

w.s. 5 and 1 through 6 and 3

tw. 4 vertical legs, pin to separate them

tw. 2 all other legs

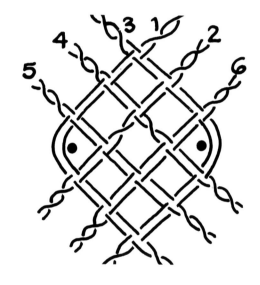

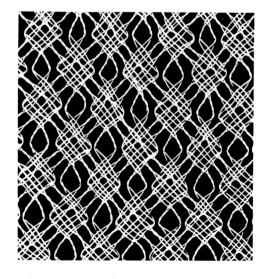

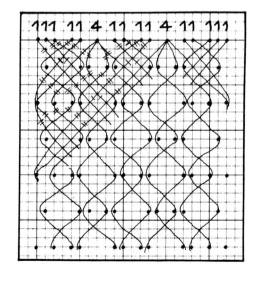

BUD STAR 5

w.s. 1 and 2 through 3 and 4

tw. 1 prs from 2 and 4

w.s. 5 through 1 and 2
w.s. 6 through 3 and 4

tw. 1 prs from 5 and 6

w.s. 1 and 2 also 3 and 4
w.s. 5 and 1 through 6 and 3

tw.4 vertical legs, pin to separate them

tw. 2 all other legs

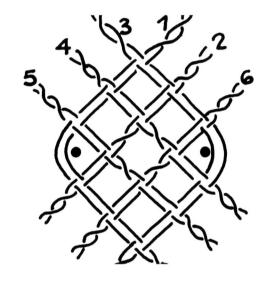

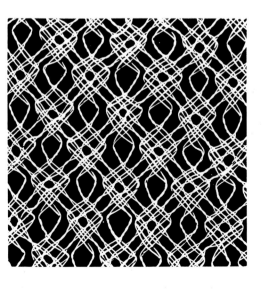

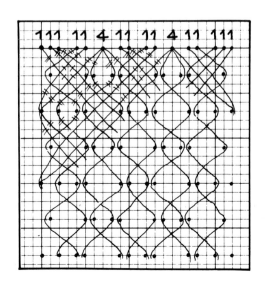

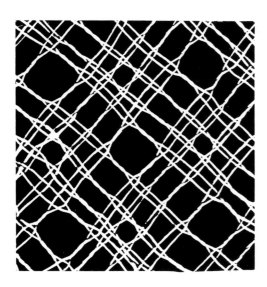

WHOLESTITCH BUD

w.s. throughout diamond

tw. 1 centre prs of diamond

pin at 4 corners only to support shape

tw. 3 between diamonds

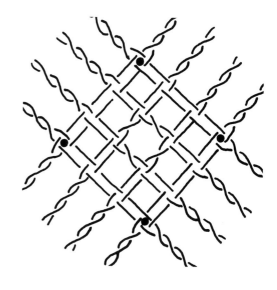

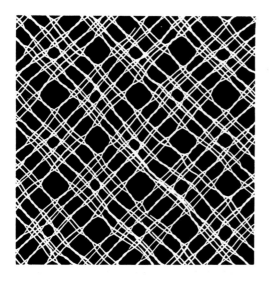

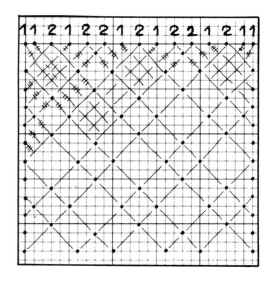

w.s., pin, w.s. at top and bottom of w.s. diamond

tw. 3 all legs between diamonds

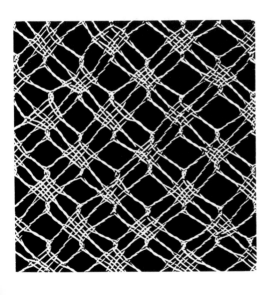

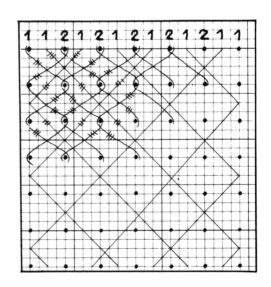

ZECCATELLO 2

w.s., tw. 1, pin, w.s. at top of spiders

w.s. throughout

tw. 2 all legs

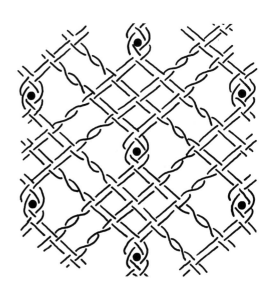

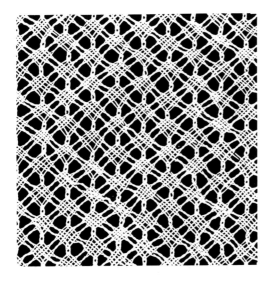

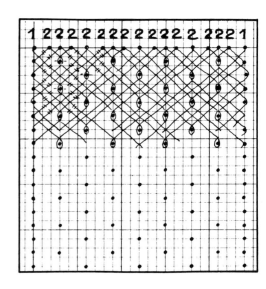

TOILE STAR 1

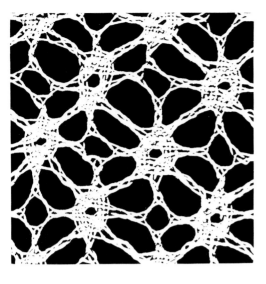

cross inner threads from 1 and 2

w.s. rt hd pr from last stitch to right
through 2 prs

w.s. 3 through 4 prs to left
w.s. 4 through 5 prs to right
take up pr from 5, w.s. to left through
2 prs
w.s. 6 to left through 2 prs and leave
w.s. 7 to right through 5 prs
w.s. pr from 1 and 2 to left through 3 prs
w.s. pr from 3 to right through 3 prs
cross last 2 prs

tw. 2 all legs

w.s. with pin in middle at intermediate
pinholes

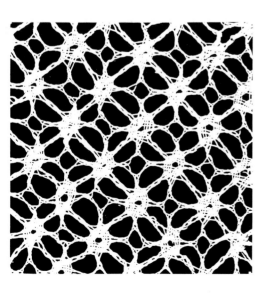

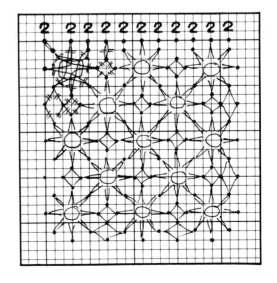

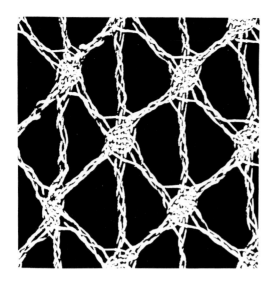

TOILE STAR 2

cross inner threads from 1 and 2

w.s. lt hd pr from last stitch to left
    through 2 prs

w.s. 3 to right through 4 prs

w.s. 4 to left through 5 prs

w.s. pr from 1 and 2 through 4 prs

w.s. pr from 3 through 2 prs

cross last 2 prs

tw. 2 all legs before and after star

w.s. with pin in middle at intermediate
    pinholes

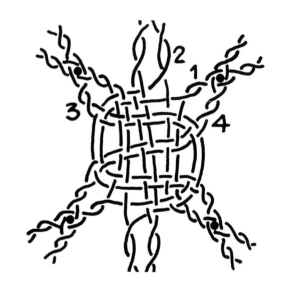

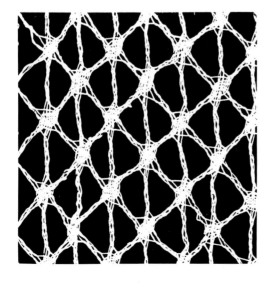

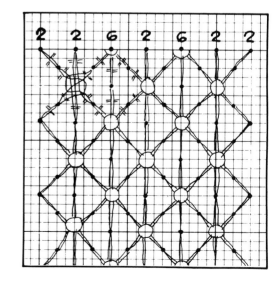

TOILE STAR 3

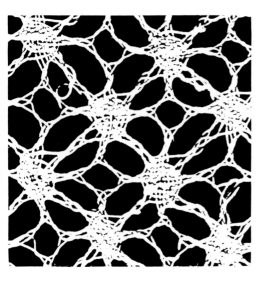

cross inner threads from 1 and 2

w.s. lt hd pr from last st. to lt through
2 prs

w.s. 3 to right through 4 prs

w.s. 4 to left through 5 prs

w.s. 5 to right through 5 prs

w.s. 6 to left through 5 prs

w.s. pr from 1 and 2 to right through
4 prs

w.s. pr from 3 to left through 2 prs

cross last 2 prs

tw. 2 all legs

w.s. with pin in middle at intermediate
pinholes

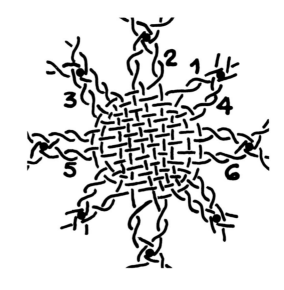

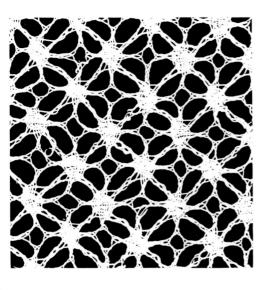

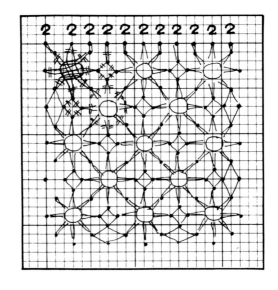

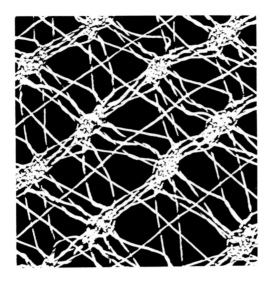

TOILE STAR 4

h.s. 2 diagonals where they cross at top
of frame, pin to support

*h.s. 3 lt hd legs in turn through lt
diagonal, giving extra tw. to legs before
new star,* repeat * to * on rt

w.s. 1 to right through 2 prs

w.s. 2 to left through 4 prs

w.s. 3 to right through 5 prs

w.s. pr from 1 to left through 4 prs

w.s. pr from 2 to right through 2 prs

tw. 1 all prs from star

h.s. pr from 2 and pr from 4

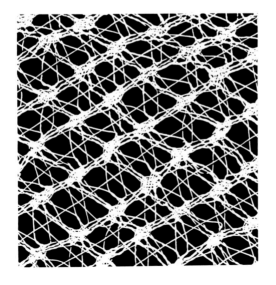

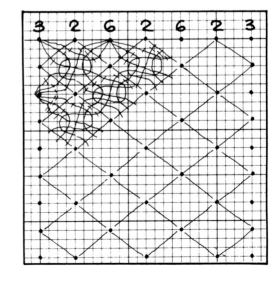

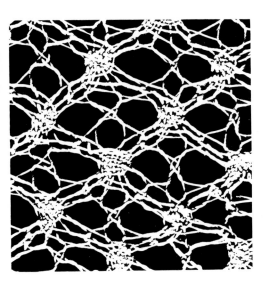

TOILE STAR 5

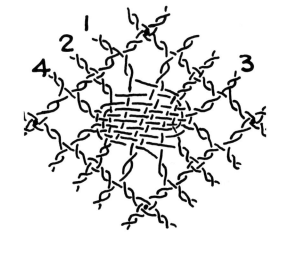

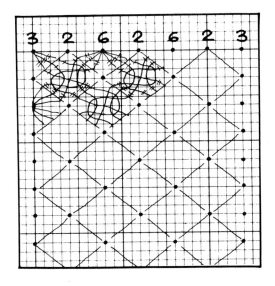

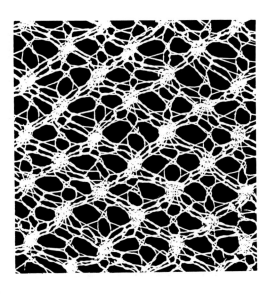

h.s., pin, h.s., tw. 1 at diagonal junctions

h.s., tw. 1, w.s., tw. 2, h.s., tw. 1 down
  diagonals

cross inner threads from 1 and 2

w.s. rt hd pr from last stitch to right
  through 2 prs

w.s. 3 to left through 4 prs

w.s. 4 to right through 5 prs

w.s. pr from 1 and 2 to left through 4 prs

w.s. pr from 3 to right through 2 prs

cross last 2 legs

tw. 2 each leg after star

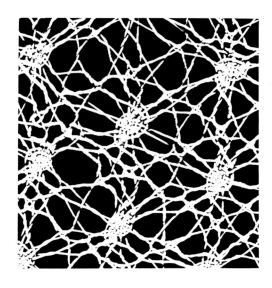

TOILE STAR 6

h.s., pin, h.s. at intersections of diagonals

h.s., tw. 1 both prs at 1
w.s., tw. 2 star side, tw. 1 diagonal at 2
h.s., tw. 1 diagonal pr only at 3
w.s., tw. 1, both prs at 4
h.s., tw. 1 diagonal pr only at 5
h.s., tw. 1 star side, prs from 3 and 4
cross inner prs from A and B
w.s. rt hd pr from last stitch through 2 prs

w.s. C to left through 4 prs
w.s. D to right through 5 prs
w.s. pr from A and B to left through 4 prs
w.s. pr from C to right through 2 prs
cross last 2 prs

tw. 2 all legs

h.s. at E and F

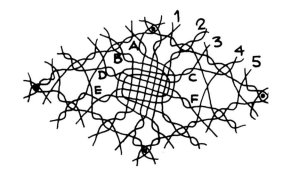

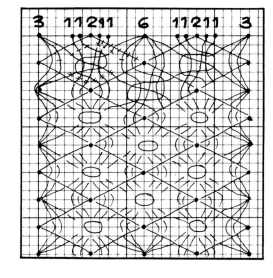

TOILE STAR IN DIAMOND FRAME

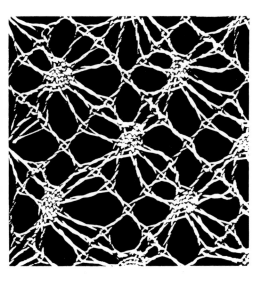

diagonals: w.s. with pin in middle
  and tw. 2

w.s. 1 to right through 3 prs

w.s. 2 to left through 4 prs

w.s. 3 to right through 5 prs

w.s. pr from 1 to left through 4 prs

tw. 2 all legs after star

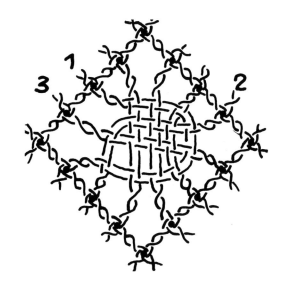

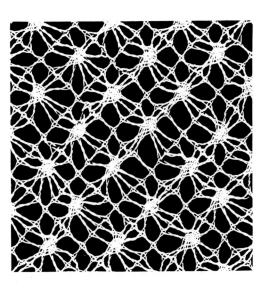

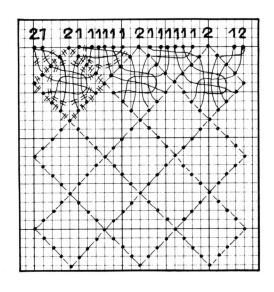

LATTICE GROUND AND STAR

spider: w.s., tw. 1, pin, w.s.

w.s., tw. 1 throughout diamond round
spider, with pin in middle of 4 corners
only

note: prs leading to spider remain
untwisted inside diamond

tw. 3 single prs and tw. 1, w.s., tw. 1 other
2 prs between diamonds

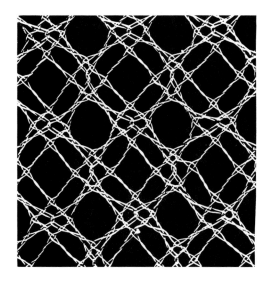

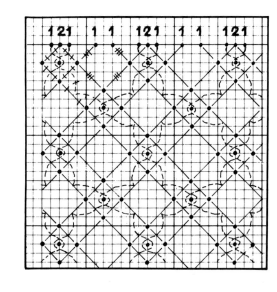

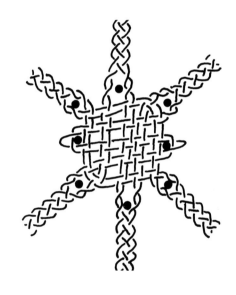

braid with double picots between stars

tw. 2 all prs before and after stars

8 pin stars in w.s. throughout

lazy join between two braids

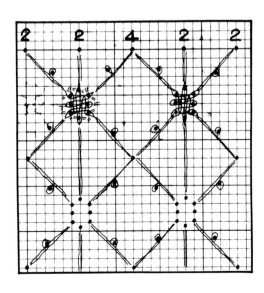

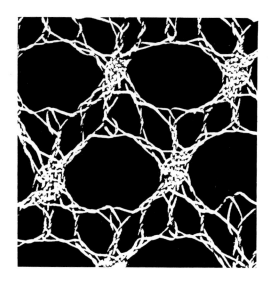

TOILE STAR WITH EXPANDED BRIDES

cross inner threads from 1 and 2

w.s. rt hd pr from last stitch to right through 2 prs

w.s. 3 to left through 4 prs

w.s. 4 to right through 5 prs

w.s. pr from 1 and 2 to left through 4 prs

w.s. pr from 3 to right through 2 prs

cross last 2 prs

tw. 2 all legs before and after star

w.s. with pin in middle at intermediate pinholes

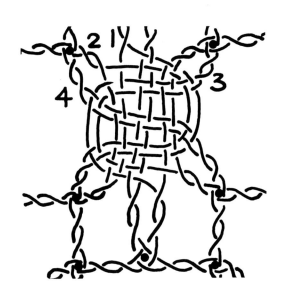

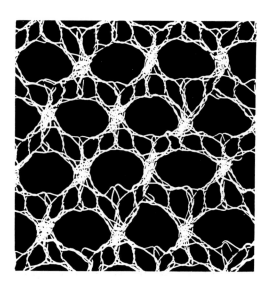

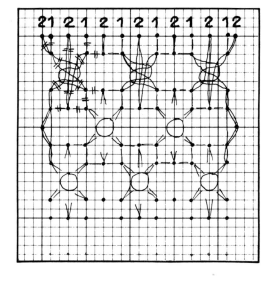

SHELL STAR WITH EXPANDED BRIDES

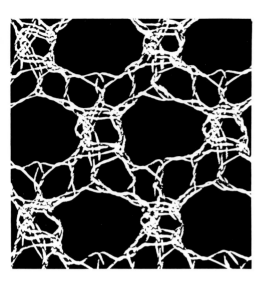

cross inner threads from 1 and 2

w.s. rt hd pr from last stitch through 2 prs
w.s. 3 to left through 4 prs
w.s. 4 to right through 3 prs, leave
w.s. pr from 1 and 2 with pr from 5

tw. 1 the 2 prs on right of star and braid
these prs x 2 and leave

w.s. pr from 3 to right through 5 prs
w.s. far rt hd pr to left through 2 prs

cross last 2 prs

tw. 2 all legs before and after star

w.s. with pin in middle at intermediate
pinholes

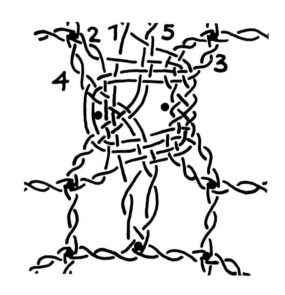

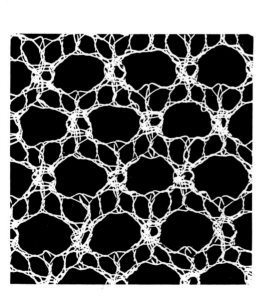

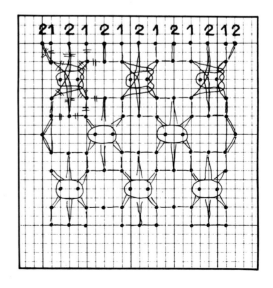

SHELL STAR 1

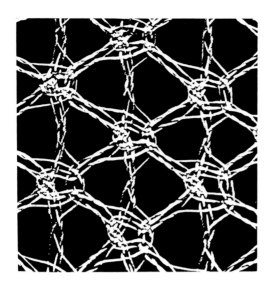

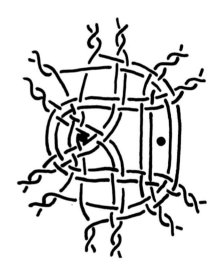

cross inner threads from lt hd pr of lt hd
  diagonal and lt hd pr from vertical
  at start of shell

w.s. throughout as diagram until last stitch,
  h.s. with rt hd diagonal and lt hd vertical

tw. 2 all diagonals and verticals

vertical legs need a pin half way down

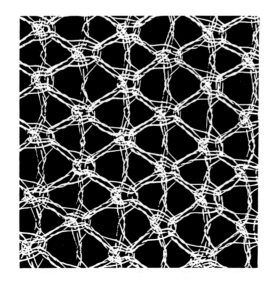

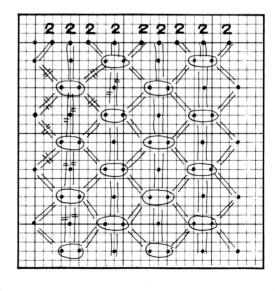

SHELL STAR 2

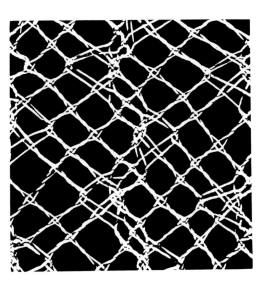

row 1 and alternate rows:
  *tw. 2 legs to start

cross inner threads of 1 and 2
w.s. 3 to rt through 2 prs
w.s., tw. 1 both prs at no. 5
cross 2 far rt hd prs and leave
w.s. 4 to right through 3 prs
w.s. 2 lt hd prs
cross inner threads of pr from 3 and
  rt hd pr from 1 and 2

tw. 2 all legs*

repeat from * to * but reversed for next
  row and each alternate row

diagonals with legs in turn w.s., tw. 2
  both prs

where diagonals meet w.s. with pin in
  middle, tw. 2

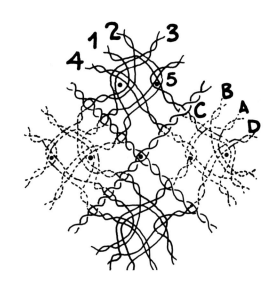

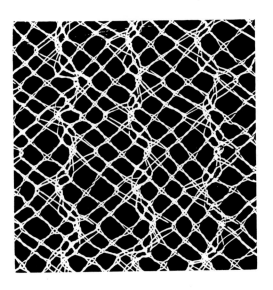

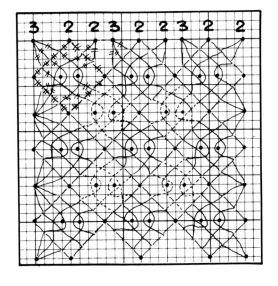

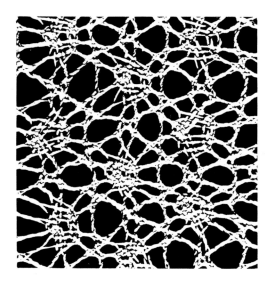

SHELL STAR 1 IN HEXAGONAL FRAME

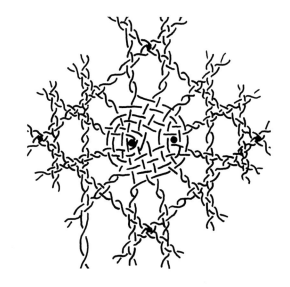

cross inner threads from lt hd pr of lt hd
diagonal and lt hd pr from vertical
at start of shell

w.s. throughout as diagram until last
stitch — h.s. with rt hd diagonal and
lt hd vertical

tw. 2 all legs from shell

tw. 1 where diagonal and vertical lines
are close, tw. 2 elsewhere

w.s. with pin in middle where diagonal
lines cross

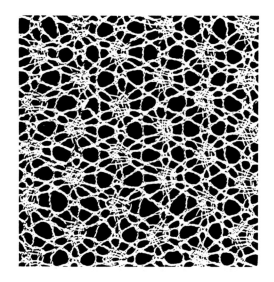

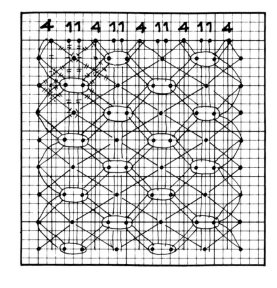

SHELL AND WHOLESTITCH BLOCKS

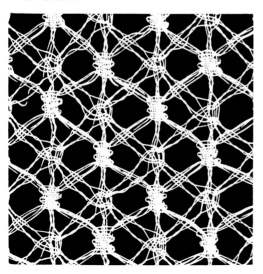

shell star:
  tw. 2 all legs, cross centre threads of
    prs 1 and 2
  w.s. rt hd pr from 1 and 2 to rt through
    2 prs
  w.s. 3 to lt through 4 prs
  w.s. prs from 4 and 2 through each
    other
  w.s. 5 to rt through 5 prs
  w.s. pr from 1 to lt through 2 prs
  cross centre 2 threads of prs from 1
    and 4

tw. 2 all legs

w.s. block:
  far rt hd pr becomes worker, w.s. back
    and forth with tw. 2 at winkie pins
    and ending at far left

tw. 2 vertical legs

diagonal legs from block to block have
  no twists

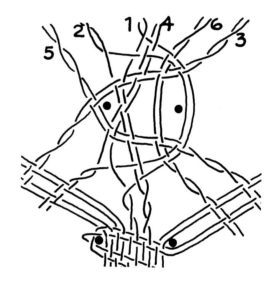

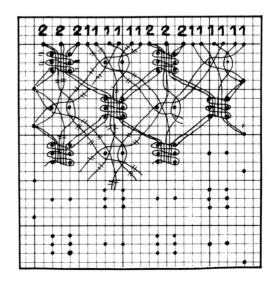

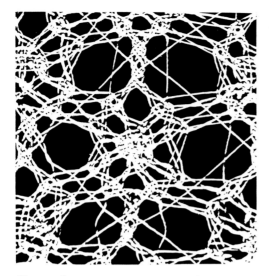

SHELL STAR IN CORD GROUND FRAME

diagonals:
    h.s. through all legs

cord ground frame round shell star:
    w.s. 2 outer prs of spider
    w.s. 2 prs from h.s. diagonals through
        first outer pr
    w.s. through each other (with pin
        in middle)
    w.s. both through inner pr

repeat both sides, tw. 1 all 8 prs

star centre:
    w.s. 1 to rt through 5 prs
    w.s. pr from 2 to lt through 3 prs
    w.s. 3 to rt through 7 prs
    w.s. pr from 4 to lt through 5 prs
    w.s. pr from 2 to rt through 3 prs
    w.s. pr from 1 to lt through 4 prs
    tw. 1 all 8 prs before completing cord
        ground frame
    tw. 1 all 8 prs before completing h.s.
        diagonals

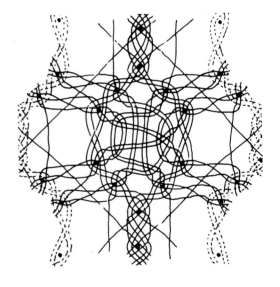

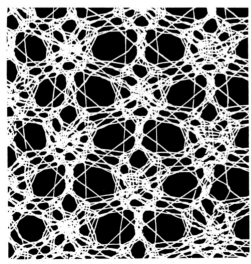

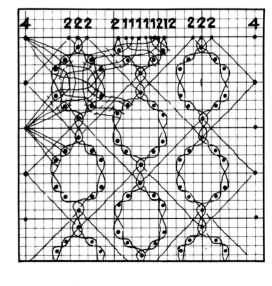

SHELL STAR AND PICOTS

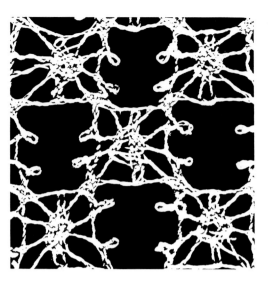

(2) shell star 1:

cross inner threads from rt hd pr of lt
hd diagonal and lt hd pr from vertical
at start of shell star

w.s. throughout as diagram until last
stitch, h.s. with rt hd diagonal and
lt hd vertical

frame, top 2 corners (4 prs):
w.s. each pr, w.s. centre prs, w.s. outside
prs, w.s. lt 2 prs, w.s. rt 2 prs, tw. 3
all prs

frame, both sides:
with outside pr make large double
picot, tw. 3 both, w.s. with vertical
pr, tw. 3 both

work shell star (see top rt corner)

first pr out of star, both sides tw. 3, w.s.
with vertical pr, tw. 3 both, make large
picot, w.s.

centre prs from star, tw. 3, pin, w.s., tw. 3

tw. 3 next prs leaving star before working
corner

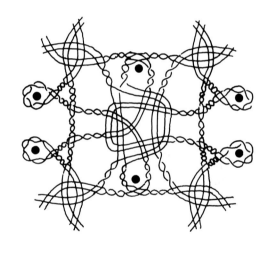

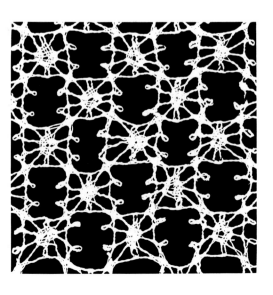

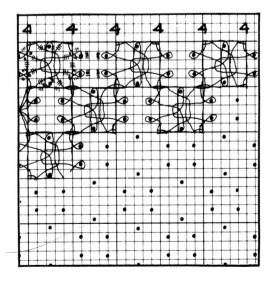

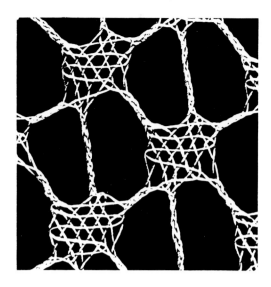

SUNSPOTS

with rt hd pr from vertical braid and lt hd pr from next diagonal pr to the right, h.s., pin, h.s. at pinhole A

h.s. lt hd pr to pinhole B (picking up 2 prs from next braid) pin, h.s. to pinholes C and D picking up extra prs left out before

h.s. to pinhole E, but *not* working last pr

h.s. to pinhole F, again *not* working last pr

close round pin with h.s.

braid all 3 legs until next sunspot

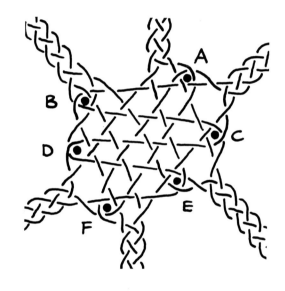

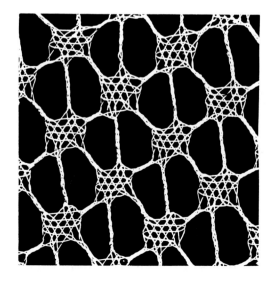

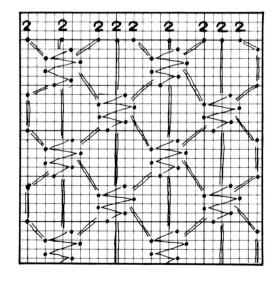

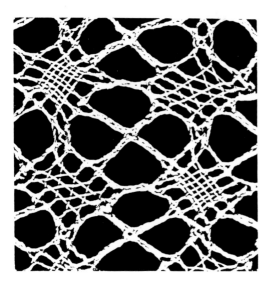

work horizontally

reverse spiders every other row

w.s., tw. 2 before and after halo

w.s. or h.s. as pattern dictates
1 pr from 5 pr side from top to bottom
through 3 prs, leave

*take next pr from 5 pr side, w.s. or
h.s. from top to bottom through 3 prs,
leave

repeat from * to * 3 more times

braid between spiders

two braids cross with lazy join

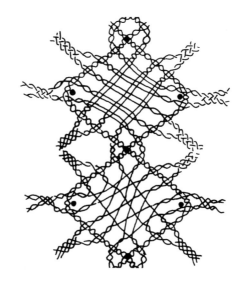

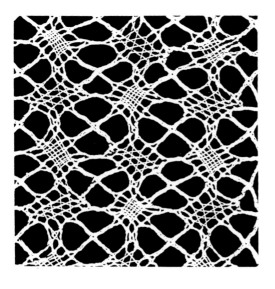

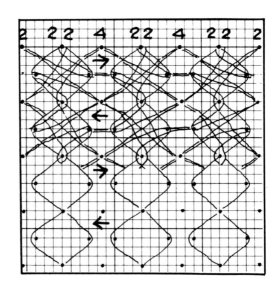

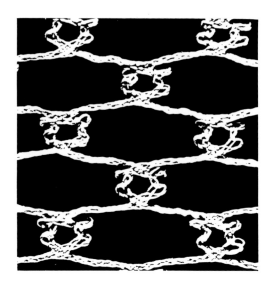

PEA WITH BRAID

braid legs

top of pea:
  w.s. 4 braid prs through each other

w.s. rt hd pr out, in, out, in, tw. 2 round
  each winkie pin

repeat rt side

w.s. 4 prs through each other

braid legs

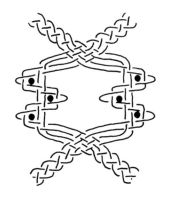

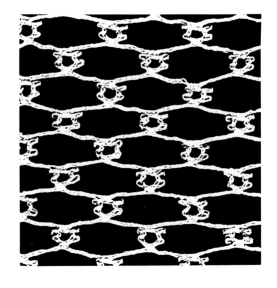

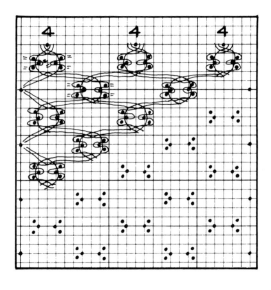

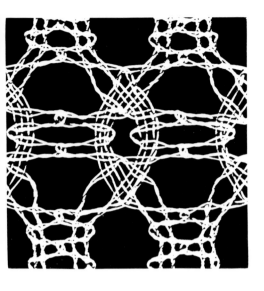

w.s. 3 lt hd prs with 3 rt hd prs
w.s. centre lt with 2 lt hd prs
tw. 2, w.s., pin, w.s. with corresponding
    pr from adjacent pea
tw. 2, w.s. rt to centre
tw. 2, pin, w.s. back as above

repeat on right side

w.s. all 3 rt hd prs with lt hd prs
pin before 2 middle prs, w.s. to hold
    shape
tw. 2 centre lt and centre rt

tw. 3 outer prs

w.s., tw. 1 back and forth until next pea

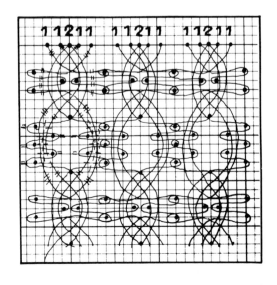

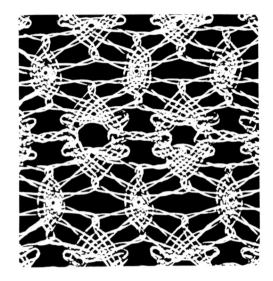

PEA WITH SPIDER

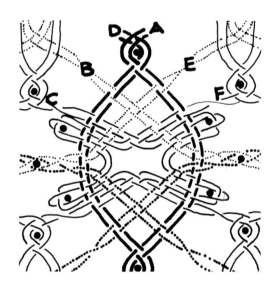

w.s., pin, w.s. prs A and D

w.s. circumference pr A with B and C
  repeat on rt side

w.s. E with B and C; F with B and C

w.s. F with E and A; pin, tw. 2, w.s. F
  back with A and E

w.s. E with A

h.s., pin, h.s. pr E with corresponding
  pr from adjacent pea

w.s. E with A and F; w.s. F with A, pin,
  tw. 2, w.s. pr F with A and E, repeat
  rt side

w.s. centre prs F with C

w.s. C with E and A; w.s. F with B and D

w.s. B with E and A; w.s. E with D

w.s., pin, w.s. circumference prs A and D

tw. 1 all prs out of pea

spiders:
  w.s., pin, w.s. at top of spiders, work
    spider with pin in middle, w.s., pin,
    w.s. at bottom

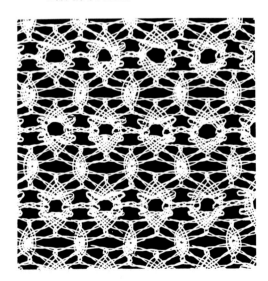

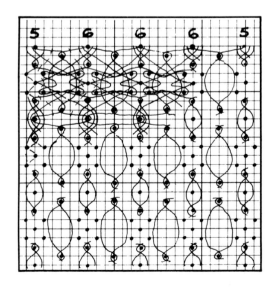

UNTWISTED FRAMED PEA

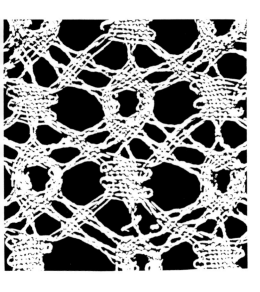

w.s. block:
   w.s. lt hd pr of centre pr with pr on its lt
   w.s. block back and forth starting at
      far rt ending far lt, tw. 2 at winkie
      pins
   tw. 2 centre prs

diagonal prs from spiders:
   tw. 2 w.s., tw. 2, w.s. through prs
   from w.s. block, tw. 2, w.s., tw. 2

spiders:
   w.s. all 6 prs through each other
   w.s. prs 1, 2, 3 and 4 through to centre
   tw. 2 prs 1 and 3, pin
   w.s. prs 1 and 2, w.s. prs 3 and 4
   w.s. prs 1 and 3 back through passives
   tw. 2 prs from 2 and 4, pin
   w.s. prs 2 and 4 back through passives
   w.s. all 6 prs through each other

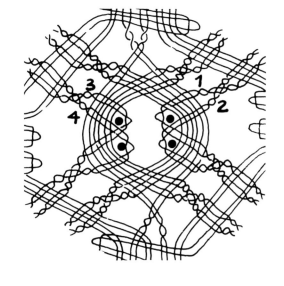

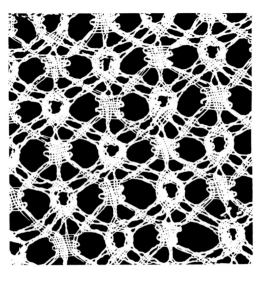

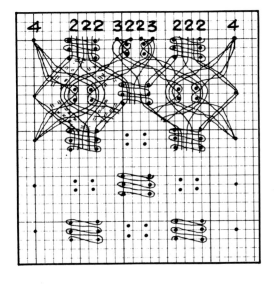

SMALL FRAMED PEA

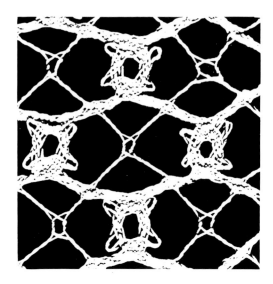

single pr frame:
  h.s., tw. 3, pin, h.s., tw. 3 and w.s.
    through 3 prs of braid, tw. 4

braid:
  w.s. outside pr through 2 prs, x 3, both
    sides

pea:
  w.s. 6 prs in order through each other

  w.s. centre 2 prs through 2 prs each side,
    tw. 3 around winkie pins

  w.s. back through 2 prs

  w.s. middle prs to outside, tw. 3 and pin

  w.s. back to centre

  w.s. 6 prs through each other

braid:
  w.s. centre prs outwards through 2 prs,
    x 3

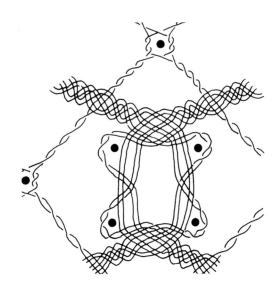

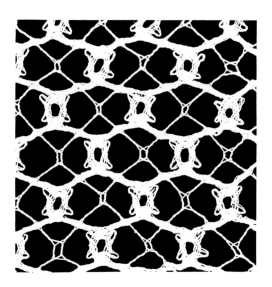

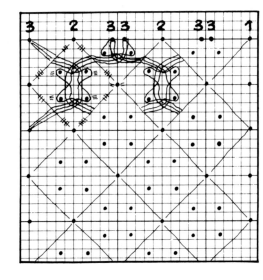

LARGE PEA WITH HALO

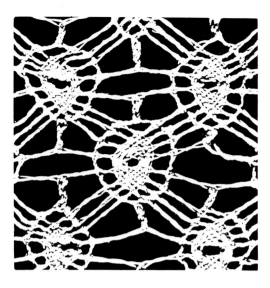

braid vertical legs
tw. 2 all other legs
tw. 2, w.s. circumference prs to left and
   right through all 8 legs
tw. 2 legs again
w.s. all 6 centre prs through each other
w.s. 2 horizontal legs to centre, tw. 2, pin,
   and w.s. back out again through 3 prs,
   tw. 2, w.s., tw. 2, both sides
w.s. all 6 centre prs through each other
tw. 2 all 6 legs
w.s., tw. 2 circumference prs back round
   all centre prs
tw. 2 all legs, except verticals — which
   are braided

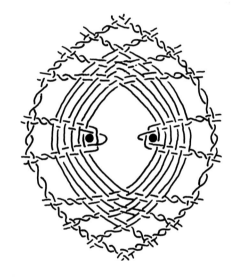

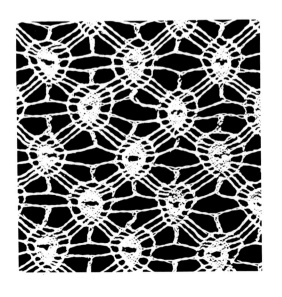

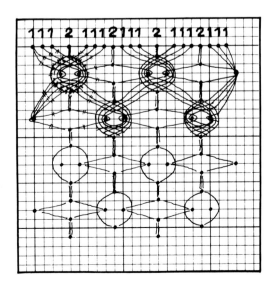

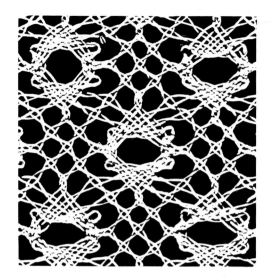

WHOLESTITCH PEA WIT EYELET

w.s., pin, w.s. prs A and D

w.s. circumference pr A with B and C
   repeat on rt side

w.s. E with B and C; F with B and C

w.s. F with E and A, pin, tw. 2, w.s. F
   back with A and E

w.s. E with A

h.s., pin, h.s. pr E with corresponding
   pr from adjacent pea

w.s. E with A and F; w.s. F with A, pin,
   tw. 2., w.s. pr F with A and E, repeat
   on rt side

w.s. centre prs F with C

w.s. C with E and A

w.s. F with B and D

w.s. D with E and A

w.s. E with D

w.s., pin, w.s. circumference prs A and D

tw. 1 all prs out of pea

h.s., pin, h.s. diagonals between

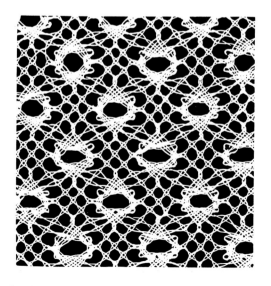

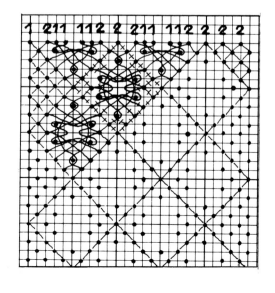